A BRIEF HISTORY OF BELFAST

Sean McMahon is a native of Derry, where he has lived for most of his life. He has more than fifty titles to his credit as author and editor, most of them in the fields of Irish history, literature and biography. He is the author of *The Bloody North: Infamous Ulster Murder Cases* (also published by The Brehon Press), and his editorial credits include the highly praised *Derry Anthology*.

A BRIEF HISTORY OF BELFAST

SEAN McMAHON

THE BREHON PRESS
BELFAST

Published by
The Brehon Press Ltd,
19 Glen Crescent
Belfast BT11 8FB
Northern Ireland

ISBN: 978 1 905474 24 0

Printed in the EU

Belfast, as all men of affairs know, stands no nonsense and lies at the head of Belfast Lough.

—EM Forster (1879–1970)

CONTENTS

Acknowledgements

I would like very much to thank those who were generous with time, help and advice: the staff of the Central Library in Derry, especially Jane Nicholas and Gerry Quinn, Paddy O'Carolan, Brian Sharkey and Brian McMahon.

1

'Knocked up from the Swamp'

WHEN MAURICE CRAIG, BELFAST'S SATIRICAL, IF loving, laureate, said that it was 'knocked up from the swamp in the last hundred years', he was exaggerating only about the date. Because of the geological nature of the terrain on which the original settlement was built, where the bottom of the U-shaped Belfast Lough meets the land, the place is boggy, too well-watered by its public and private rivers, the Lagan, the Blackstaff, the Farset, the Milewater and the Connswater to the east – not a site where one with any sense would choose to build a city.

Its precise geographical location as given by one of its earliest historians, George Benn (1801–82) in his *History of the Town of Belfast*, written when he was 18, is 54°36' N and 5°54' W. Ice-Age modification played its part in the creation of the sloblands, leaving a soft, sleechy plain in the gap of the hills. The closeness and beetling height (between 1,000 and 1,500 feet) of those to the northwest – the Black Mountain, Divis (the Irish name of which, *Dubhais*, also means a black mountain), Squire's Hill and Cave Hill – discouraged natural expansion in that direction, and the Castlereagh and Holywood hills were high enough at 500 feet to prevent easy growth to the east. To the south were thick oak forests covering, as we have noted, soft, even swampy, terrain. As a seventeenth-century chronicler rather fancifully put it:

> So dense were the woods in the time of our forefathers, that a man might make his way from MacArt's fort at Belfast to Lisnagarvagh, without his foot touching aught than the tops of the trees.[1]

The nucleus of the future city was in early times no more than a handy sand bar that allowed passage to the other side of the lough at low tide. From prehistoric times hunters and gatherers could make their way across, if not dryshod, at least without having to swim. The most obvious relic of these proto-inhabitants is the Giant's Ring, the large (7.4 acres, 640 feet in diameter), circular Neolithic enclosure about four miles south of the city that has an impressive dolmen, slightly off-centre above a passage grave. MacArt's promontory fort is a similar relic of ancient habitation. The passageway gave the place its title: *Béal Feirste* – the mouth of, or perhaps more geologically accurate, the approach to the sandbank ford – and it was from it that the hidden River Farset that runs beneath High Street took its name.

For thousands of years the inhabitants of the region did not develop towns, preferring to use a different social structure, with solitary homesteads, a few shacks built in the shadow of defensive forts and the monastic settlements that were the only 'towns' of Gaelic Ireland. The chief of these monasteries in the region were Bangor and Movilla, a mile east of present-day Newtownards. Bangor, founded by Comgall (c.516–601) in 555, and ruled by him for 50 years, was the seminary of such illustrious saints as Columban, Gall and Malachy. Movilla, a mere five miles away, was founded by Finnian (c.493–579) and it became the great Irish centre for biblical studies.

The eventual settlement was well-named since the sandy ford was the defining element. To cross from what later came to be known as Antrim to Down would otherwise have required a boat or meant a considerable detour to the south. For a millennium and a half the place slept its way through the turmoil of dynastic struggle that saw the fall of the Ulaid, the tribes east of the Bann (Ulster's north–

south axis), the growth of such pan-Celtic kingdoms as the Dál Riata, which regarded the stormy North Channel as an inner sea, the harrying of the lough by Viking raiders, and even the coming of the Anglo-Normans, who preferred Carrickfergus, building one of their great keeps at the harbour of that already existing town.

That sleep was interrupted from time to time: as early as the seventh century tribal battles were fought there between the Pictish Cruithin and the Ulaid. Some kind of primitive structure seems to have been established then, its main purpose being surveillance. It was an obvious site for keeping an eye on traffic between Down and Antrim. There were probably some ancillary dwellings for service purposes and there is evidence for the existence of an early church, the Shankill (*Sean–Chill* or 'old church') near the structure. John de Courcy (d. 1190), the freebooting founder of Anglo-Norman Ulster, built a stronger structure, perhaps at Castle Junction or further down High Street where the Farset meets the Lagan. There must have been some habitation associated with the place because he referred to it as 'Le Ford'.

Since a substantial building now existed at the sandbank it inevitably became involved in the many local wars from the twelfth until the sixteenth century. The Anglo-Normans did not complete their conquest, perhaps unfortunately in the light of later history. As Sean O'Faolain puts it in his excellent monograph *The Irish* (1969), 'The Normans did not give to the Irish the benefits of their own laws.' Their instinct for rootedness and urbanisation ultimately affected only the peripheral lands of the east, the 'Pale' and a few Ulster outposts, Lecale and Ards, but they taught the Irish how to make and live in towns. They failed in Ulster because the native system was as complicated, as subtle and as nicely fitted to the needs of the native Irish as their trim castle-keeps were for the invaders. And they made the mistake of regarding the Irish as barbarous and uncivilised because their psychology and sociology were greatly different from that of these people from the neighbouring island.

As the Anglo-Norman power waned the native Irish reasserted

themselves and at different times during the thirteenth, fourteenth and fifteenth centuries, 'Le Ford' was attacked, occupied, destroyed and rebuilt. Those years saw the rise and eventual supremacy of the O'Neills, a hegemony that was characterised by typical internecine conflict.

The castle of Belfast was the scene of recurring struggles between the Tyrone O'Neills and those of Clandeboye. These east Ulster O'Neills, known in Irish as *Clann Aoidh Buidhe* ('the family of blonde Hugh'), took their name from Hugh O'Neill, who died in 1283. By the end of the fourteenth century they were the overlords of large sections of south Antrim and north Down (where the name is still preserved). The sept was noted for its cooperation with the residual Anglo-Norman power. Belfast continued to play its literally pivotal part in the Clandeboye territory since it linked the two stretching arms that those O'Neills controlled. The castle was attacked by the senior O'Neills (those of Tyrone) in 1476 and by *their* hereditary adversaries, the O'Donnells, in 1489. The 'Great' Earl of Kildare, Garret More Fitzgerald, the 8th Earl, who was Henry VII's lord deputy, on punitive expeditions against the Clandeboye O'Neills sacked Belfast in 1503 and 1512.

These small local wars were part of the everyday life of sixteenth-century Ireland and no great notice was taken. Then Henry VIII's need for a healthy male heir (if for no other reason) caused him to divorce his first wife and break with Rome. This apostasy of the most Roman Catholic of countries changed the whole history not only of England but Ireland as well. The king was rather less detached about the western island than his father and none of Garret More's family persuaded him of their strength or political nous. He had himself declared king of Ireland in 1541 at a ceremony in Dublin with the approval of the Dublin parliament. The Irish clan chieftains, as was their wont, paid little attention and in Ulster the declaration was disregarded. It was not until the English Reformation had taken hold and Scotland become largely Presbyterian that the presence of the *Gall* (as the Irish called all foreigners) became intrusive.

The reign of Elizabeth I (1533–1603) saw the most serious and successful attempts at colonisation. Ireland had always been a perplexing neighbour but now it presented itself as a fine place for conquest and exploitation. It was also potentially a largely undefended back entrance to the forces of the counter-reformation, especially those of powerful Catholic Spain, and the threat of such a return of popery and the possible dethronement of the queen gave the perpetrators of the imposing of English 'civility' a veneer of righteousness.

It was Walter Devereux, the ruthless 1st Earl of Essex (1541–76), who first saw the potential of Belfast for his and England's gain. In 1573 he described it as a

> place meet for a corporate town, armed with all commodities, as a principal haven, wood and good ground, standing also upon a border and a place of great importance for service…

A similar description would be applied to the western city of 'Derrie' in 1604 by James I (1566–1625), as he made the officials of the London city guilds an offer they dared not refuse. He described the city that would be called Londonderry in tribute to the source of its investments as 'a place very convenient and fit to be made both a town of war and of merchandise'. Then it seemed a better prospect than Belfast. It had been a monastic foundation since the middle of the sixth century, the site of the Teampull Mór in the twelfth, and now a busy city under the care of Sir Henry Docwra (1560–1631) while Belfast's development suffered endless delays. An attempt to take control of it in 1571 by Sir Thomas Smith, who came with letters patent from Elizabeth I to claim the Belfast territory and other lands in Down and Antrim from the Clandeboye O'Neills, whose holdings stretched from Whitehead to Bangor, was not successful. The O'Neills, under their chieftain Sir Brian Mac Phelim O'Neill (d. 1574), not surprisingly did not agree with the plan and soon dispatched Smith and his inadequate army, killing his son in the process.

The Clandeboye territory had been surrendered by and regranted to the O'Neills (as the Tudor terms of loyalty demanded) in 1552 and Sir Brian was naively dismayed when Elizabeth assigned part of it to Smith, contravening a previous agreement made in 1568 with Sir Henry Sidney, the lord deputy, to deliver the castle to him on condition that he build a bridge over the tidal part of 'Le Ford' and develop the area's economical potential.

Devereux was a different kind of colonist. His name is remembered in Antrim with hatred for his slaughter in 1575 of all the McDonnell women and children in Rathlin where they had been sent for safety by the clan chief, Sorley Boy (c.1505–90). In this expedition his most enthusiastic lieutenant was the famous Sir Francis Drake (c.1540–1596). With typical efficient Elizabethan treachery he came to an understanding with Sir Brian O'Neill and invited him to stay with friends and followers at the castle – the most substantial element in the place. They were all killed except Sir Brian, his wife and brother, who were taken to Dublin where they were hanged and quartered.

The queen, in one of her occasional benevolent or vacillatory moods, withdrew support from Devereux. He died of dysentery in Dublin in 1576. There was to be no substantial English presence in Clandeboye until the beginning of the Nine Years' War during which Hugh O'Neill (1550–1616), the chief prince of Ulster and Earl of Tyrone, almost finished English power in Ulster. That dream faded with his defeat at Kinsale in 1603 and James I, the new king, was determined finally to settle the Ulster question by plantation.

2

The Chichesters

A FORM OF UNOFFICIAL PLANTATION WAS already in operation. It was organised by a typical Tudor magnate, who was a successful army commander and a resolute acquirer of land, if somewhat less astute as a businessman. This was Arthur Chichester (1563–1625), later Baron Chichester of Belfast, and founder of the Donegall family who by the late eighteenth century owned more land than any other family in Ireland.

As well as ten locations in present-day Belfast using the name Chichester, there are 18 with the name Donegall. This is perfectly appropriate since if the city had a founder it was the Baron of Belfast. Like Drake, with whom he served as captain of a galleon on an expedition to the West Indies, he was born in Devon but fled to Ireland when he was 20. As an undergraduate at Oxford he had a violent altercation with a tax official. The incident did not seriously affect his career. He helped defeat the Spanish Armada when he was 25 and was the ablest second-in-command of Earl Mountjoy (1563–1606), the lord deputy, against Hugh O'Neill in the Nine Years' War, carrying out the scorched earth policy which devastated O'Neill's Tyrone lands. Knighted by Elizabeth in 1595 he was created commander of Carrickfergus in 1598.

When Ulster was left virtually leaderless in 1607 after the departure of O'Neill, Rory O'Donnell (1575–1608) of Tír Conaill and Cúchonnacht Maguire (?–1608) of Fermanagh, James I decided to impose the final solution to the problem of Ulster's refusal to conform. In six of the Ulster counties – Tyrone, Coleraine (later Londonderry), Donegal, Armagh, Fermanagh and Cavan – lands taken to be forfeited by the original chieftains because of their treason were to be parcelled out to undertakers from England, Wales and Scotland. Chichester, who had been granted Belfast and large tracts of the contiguous lands of south Antrim in 1603 for his military services, was one of the main architects of the scheme. By 1605 he had become lord deputy himself, serving until 1616, making him the official with the longest tenure. Already he had begun a private plantation scheme, filling much of the old Clandeboye territory with hard-working, austere Scots Presbyterians. These he correctly surmised were not likely to rent back the land to the evicted Irish holders, as a number of the English adventurers had done. In a way his personal plantation scheme became a template for the officially planted counties; he was able to demonstrate that the initiative could be made to work.

When the fiery and unwise Sir Cahir O'Doherty (1587–1608), the very young protégé of Docwra, was killed after rising against the English – a revolt inspired partly as a consequence of Cahir's treatment by Chichester – with the inexorable logic of the period, the O'Doherty territories, comprising the large peninsula of Inishowen in Donegal, were given to the lord deputy. It was this grant, along with the contemporary spelling of the county, which gave the name to Chichester's descendants, who were Earls of Donegall from 1647, and the source of Donegall Place et al.

With the lands of O'Doherty and the Clandeboye O'Neills in his possession, and serving as the king's chief minister in Ireland, as well as overseer of the Ulster plantation, Chichester had not a great deal of time to attend to his town of Belfast. When in Ulster he lived in the mansion he had built for himself at Joymount in Carrickfergus, then still called Knockfergus. It was there that he and his family were buried, as a memorial tomb in St Nicholas's church reminds us, and impressed Louis MacNeice (1907–63), who spent part of his boyhood there:

> The Chichesters knelt in marble at the end of a transept
> With ruffs round their necks, their portion sure.

However, the clearest mark of 'civility' was the neat, well-run town and Chichester decided to make Belfast an exemplar.

He rebuilt the castle and encouraged Protestant settlers to make their homes in the area. By 1611 the government inspectors were impressed by the town's progress and reported:

> The towne of Bealfast is plotted out in a good forme, wherein are many fameleys of English, Scotish and some Manksmen already inhabitinge, of which some are artificers who have buylte good tymber houses with chimneys after the fashion of the English palle, and one inn with very good Lodgings which is a great comforte to the travellers in those partes.

Chichester was in fact preparing a town for his descendants, a town that would become almost a private possession. Two years later, on 27 April 1613, in a blatantly political move it was 'incorporated' and as such entitled to send two Protestant members to the parliament in Dublin. The Old English of the Pale refused to give up their Catholicism and, on the instructions of James I, 40 new boroughs including Belfast were created to ensure a Protestant majority. Political chicanery in Ulster did not begin with gerrymandering in the 1920s.

As far as internal politics were concerned, Chichester virtually owned the new borough. Its nominal administration was in the hands of a corporation consisting of the 'lord of the castle', a deputy known as the constable, a 'sovereign' (the equivalent of the later 'mayor', that coming from the Latin *major*, meaning simply 'greater'), and twelve free burgesses appointed for life. They chose the sovereign yearly on the feast of St John (24 June) from a short list of their own members nominated by Chichester (and the head of the family in later years). The original incorporation listed the first set of 'free burgesses' and it was these officials who along with the sovereign nominated the members of parliament.

There was a further not very significant set of townspeople called 'the commonalty' or 'free commoners'. These were inhabitants of the town who had paid a fee to the sovereign in exchange for certain privileges that were vaguely concerned with the finances of the town. The real advantage that the free commoners had was in the matter of market tolls.

The growth of the borough in the seventeenth century was as sluggish as in the sixteenth. Any economic development was in the field of marketing rather than manufacturing. The borough, because of its position and the easing of communications, became a natural market centre, even though it was no larger and no busier than such other east Ulster towns as Lisburn and Newry. The building of the 2,562-foot Long Bridge, with its 21 arches, begun in 1682, gave permanent access, linking County Down and County Antrim, and increased trade considerably. The free commoners began to object to incursions by alien traders who because of their mobility often avoided paying the tolls.

The Chichesters had everything to gain from the economic development of their fief but succession tended to be indirect with nephews inheriting as often as sons. The first Arthur's nephew, also called Arthur (1606–75), was made Earl of Donegall in 1647 and he, a supporter of Charles I (1600–1649) in the Civil War, found it advisable to stay with the future Charles II (1630–1685) until after the Restoration in 1660. He made up for lost time when he came to live in the borough. He enlarged the castle and laid out gardens, orchards and pleasant walks that pleased William III (1650–1702) of glorious, pious and immortal memory when in June 1690 he stayed there on his way to the Boyne.

The middle decades of the seventeenth century in Ireland were violent, bloody and horribly confused. From 1641, when stirred on by impoverished Ulster Irish landowners some dispossessed Catholics were encouraged to attack the new settlers, until the Restoration of Charles II in 1660, there was much warfare and continually shifting allegiances though Belfast emerged from the chaos relatively unscathed. There were few Catholics in the area in 1641 when the rising began.

The plantation in Chichester territory was notably different from that in the formally escheated territory of the six westerly counties. As we have seen, the borough had a population of English and Scots encouraged to settle there by the first Chichester. In the rising of 1641 the town stayed safe though the insurgents came close enough for their campfires to be seen by its people. When the threat of incursion abated, the corporation, urged by the lord of the castle, Edward Chichester, the first Arthur's brother, built an earthwork round the town to compensate for the lack of protective stone walls. This *rampier*, as they called it, enclosed the borough in 1642. It stretched from the south end of present-day Corporation Street at the river's edge round by North Street, Queen Street, College Square and May Street where it met the Lagan again. (The river was regarded as an effective defence.) The town had not yet moved into Down, though the building of the Long Bridge inevitably stimulated growth to the east.

The population was Protestant with a majority of Presbyterians, who had come from Lowland Scotland. With the outbreak of several British Civil Wars in the 1640s, Belfast's population was divided about allegiance. The Chichesters stood by Charles I but many of the townspeople favoured the forces of Parliament. It was because of the Irish rebellion that enmity between the king and Parliament increased. Both sides wanted to control the soldiers sent to crush the Irish insurgents, and the Confederate War (1641 –53), a development of the insurrection, amounted to a kind of Irish civil war, a replica of the English one that lasted from 1642 until 1646, ending with the trial and condemnation of Charles I.

Oliver Cromwell (1599–1658), having defeated the Royalist forces with his effective New Model Army – 30,000 strong – landed at Ringsend in Dublin on 15 August 1649 and carried out the seventeenth-century equivalent of a *Wehrmacht* blitzkrieg between then and the 26th of the following May, breaking the back of the Confederate forces, though that war persisted until 1653.

Throughout this turmoil Belfast managed to escape serious violence though it was occupied at various times by commanders from different sides in the very confusing conflict. The first was the Scots general Robert Monro, who arrived at Carrickfergus in April 1642 to protect his fellow countrymen from the insurgents. Taking the side of Parliament at the outbreak of the English Civil War he obtained possession of Belfast on 14 May 1644, finding it undefended. He remained in the town until 1648 but like other Scots opposed the Parliamentary forces, having refused to obey orders to hand it over to the Roundheads. The town was besieged by the Parliamentary commander, Colonel Robert Venables, and it capitulated after a four-day siege, on 1 October 1649.

It was General George Monck (1608–70), once a Royalist who had accepted Parliamentary commands in 1647, and yet another town commander in Belfast, who ended the long and barren Commonwealth at the death of Cromwell, who had called himself the Lord Protector, and arranged for the return of Charles II and the re-establishment of the monarchy in 1660.

The small east Ulster town prospered slowly during the Commonwealth and more rapidly after 1660. The Chichester family was back in the castle and the younger Arthur benefited financially from his fidelity to the Merry Monarch. As already stated he improved the castle's amenity and looked benevolently on the borough's growing prosperity. He did not do much more; it was the townspeople, mainly Scots, who began the slow growth that burgeoned by the end of the eighteenth century.

Belfast has for many years had the reputation of a city cursed by sectarian dissension. In the seventeenth century the clash of religions or ideologies involved Presbyterianism and Anglicanism. The latter kept faithful to Charles I before and during the English Civil War and that was the attitude of the Chichesters, who still 'owned' the borough. Yet it was the first Arthur who was responsible for the large influx of Lowland Scots. They had, by and large, the virtues of frugality, industry and patience that made them ideal colonists. Their stern religion, with its certainties of their being the Almighty's elect, was both comfort and stimulus. In the shifting patterns of allegiances they found themselves for the king but against his policies and beliefs; they were horrified at the regicide and eventually at odds with the Parliamentary Puritans. Even before the outbreak of serious trouble Belfast Presbyterians were called before an Anglican tribunal, led by the Bishop of Down, to explain their refusal to subscribe to certain Anglican doctrines, including the authority of the episcopacy.

Catholics were hardly considered: one survey made in 1708 by George Macartney, then sovereign, on the instruction of the authorities in Dublin reported:

> We have not amongst us within the town above seven Papists, and by return made by the High Constable there is not above 150 papists in the whole Barony.

The barony in question included Belfast Upper and Upper and Lower Castlereagh. Catholics made themselves as inconspicuous as possible when they heard of the massacre of their co-religionists in Islandmagee in 1642 when it was believed that Monro's Scots singled out children for attention with the cry, 'Nits make lice.' From the point of view of Belfast's Presbyterians and Episcopalians the minuscule Popish population were objects of little interest and no persecution. The practice even of the Episcopalian Church was designated 'low'; the high church practices of England with its saints (including the Blessed Virgin), clergy called priests and confessional boxes would have seemed very 'Romish' to the austere Church of Ireland.

By comparison Presbyterianism was even more rigid and intolerant of all other religions. On 15 February 1649 Belfast Presbyterians dismissed the edict of the essentially republican Parliament allowing religious toleration. They insisted that 'universal toleration of all religions' was 'directly repugnant to the law of God'.[1] The Presbyterian objection was excoriated by no less a person as the poet John Milton (1608–74), who had just been appointed as Cromwell's Latin Secretary (the equivalent of today's Foreign Secretary). He referred to Belfast as

> …a barbarous nook… Belfast, a place better known by the name of a late barony than by the fame of these men's doctrine or ecclesiastical deeds, whose obscurity till now never came to our hearing.

Catholics did begin to play a part with the death of Charles II in 1685 and the coming to the throne of James II (1633 –1701). Charles had been inclined to tolerance and was presumed to have died in the Catholic Church but he was acutely aware of his position as king and acted accordingly. He was publicly inactive (though privately concerned) during the anti-Catholic persecutions engendered by the rabid clergyman Titus Oates (1649–1705). His younger brother, by contrast, had none of his elder's political wisdom. Seemingly unaware of the precariousness of his position in an almost entirely Protestant Britain, he began to replace existing senior officials with Catholics. When he became king in 1685 the Belfast Corporation made a fulsome declaration of loyalty with a certain nervousness about what changes a Catholic monarch might make in the borough. In 1688 it had a new charter. Half the burgesses were to be Catholic and since there were very few Catholics in Belfast, and none with any property, the new burgesses had to be imported.

It was with considerable relief that the inhabitants greeted the arrival of the Protestant William III, James's son-in-law, after what some historians have called the 'Bloodless Revolution'. It was not bloodless in Ireland and the names of Jacobite defeats, Derry, Aughrim, Enniskillen and the Boyne, chronological order sacrificed to euphony, have been iconic for Ulster Protestants ever since.

William III's terms for the Jacobite surrender at Limerick were generous and, with the tradition of toleration of his native Holland, he did what he could for the many Catholics who found themselves without leaders with the departure of the Wild Geese.[2] It was the small but powerful group of Protestant Irish landowners who controlled the Dublin parliament who imposed the Popery Laws that were intended to make permanent the seventeenth-century land settlements. In this they were supported by Anne (1665–1714), William's sister-in law and James's other daughter, who became queen on William's unexpected death in 1702.

Her upbringing had been strongly High Church and she was nearly as intolerant of Presbyterianism as Catholicism. She reintroduced the oath of supremacy, which William had allowed to lapse and which was anathema to the Presbyterian majority in Belfast. William's Dutch Protestantism was closer to theirs than to Anglicanism. He had doubled the *regium donum* ('royal bounty') instituted by Charles II in 1672 to help pay Presbyterian clergymen up to £1,200. Both James II and Anne had forbidden its payment for different but similar religious reasons. The reign of Anne also saw the most rigorous penal enactments against Catholics that were to remain on the statute book for more than 90 years, though the severity of their application varied from place to place. They had almost no impact in Belfast because of the paucity of numbers and the lack of any perceived threat. In 1795 it was Belfast Protestants who first petitioned parliament for a removal of the penal disabilities.

Though still nonconformist, Presbyterians saw some relief with the accession of George I. The *regium donum* was further increased to £1,600 in 1718. Belfast was becoming a town with a majority of dissenting Scots rather than English Episcopalians, especially since the tenor of the eighteenth century was of enlightenment and toleration – except, of course, towards Catholics. The town, James II's nominees having been ousted by Chichester, was still a Chichester fief. The family suffered two setbacks at the beginning of the eighteenth century. The third Lord Donegall was killed fighting for the Duke of Marlborough (1650–1722), Queen Anne's commander-in-chief, in Spain in 1706 at the age of 40 when the fourth earl (1695–1757) was only eleven years of age. The fourth earl's powers were taken over by a board of trustees. His father had taken his civic responsibilities seriously, initiating reclamation work along the Lagan. The Chichester family seemed to have a tradition of naming at least one son Arthur after the founder of the dynasty since it was given to the third, fourth and fifth earls. Arthur, the fourth earl, was not only too young at his inheritance, he was also regarded as being weak in the head. Either way he had not the capacity to act successfully as lord of the castle.

This caused a great deal of anger and frustration for the merchants of the town and the corporation tried to have the fourth earl declared incompetent. Most of the mercantile and other improvements in the town had been done by the business people there in cooperation for mutual benefit, and not by the ruling family. The quay, for example, needed maintenance and the necessary channel through the mud and sand kept clear if the town was to fulfil its manifest destiny as a port of trade. The Lord Chancellor would not hear of one of his peers declared an imbecile, though Arthur's competence was established by only a narrow margin. It was something of a relief when he died in 1757, having for most of his life been that well-known phenomenon of Irish history – an absentee landlord; but nearly half a century of stagnation had resulted from his mental condition.

The other calamity that befell the family during the fourth earl's tenure was the destruction by fire on 24 April 1708 of the family home, Belfast Castle. Three of Arthur's sisters perished in the blaze and one of Belfast's few significant buildings became a ruin.

Arthur's successor, his nephew Arthur (1739–99), continued the absenteeism. He built a mansion at Fisherwick in Staffordshire, with a landscape designed by the famous 'Capability' Brown (1716–83), a fitting residence for the largest landowner in Ireland. He increased rents and sold tenancies over the heads of the holders, a practice that produced an early movement of agrarian protest, called the 'Hearts of Steel' or 'Steelboys'. Their activities that arose out of their quarrel with Donegall in County Antrim in 1770 spread in 1771–2 to Derry, Down and Armagh, becoming a general protest movement about rents, evictions and the price of food. In 1770, a band of 500 Steelboys invaded Belfast and had one of their leaders released from prison after a threat to burn the town, which still had a number of wooden houses. The Hearts of Steel, with a membership exclusively Protestant, was to have a kind of reincarnation 25 years later as the Orange Order.

Donegall had promised to improve the harbour and channel but became interested instead in completing the Lagan Navigation. Canals were important because of the poor state of Irish roads; water was preferred for the transport of heavy or fragile goods. The earliest, which connected Carlingford Lough with Portadown (1731–42), anticipated the first English canal by 20 years. (As we had long suspected, the first navvies were Irish.) The Lagan Navigation that linked Belfast with Lough Neagh was completed in the 1780s.

According to Donegall's obituary printed in the *Belfast News Letter*, then in its 63rd year (and still printed daily in the twenty-first century), he 'laid out above £60,000 in the Lagan Navigation and the Public Buildings in the Town'. Though Ireland's oldest newspaper (1737) does not hint at it, this outlay contributed more to a satisfaction of Donegall's vanity than to the mercantile health of the town. He did at least settle one source of discontent: the original property leases were only for a term of 31 years and as such gave no encouragement towards improvement or even proper maintenance. The 99-year leases that Donegall did grant were on very expensive terms and hedged about with conditions. They were mainly for rebuilding and specified height and minimum thickness of walls of dwellings. They also required sash windows and slate roofs. In spite of the expense the leases paved the way for the great leap forward that did not find its full force until the nineteenth century. Even so the population increased in the second half of the eighteenth century from 8,500 in 1750 to 20,000 in 1800.

Donegall celebrated the birth of his first son in 1769 by building a market-house and assembly rooms – those necessary adjuncts to bourgeois society, as any reader of Jane Austen can verify. He also provided free the land for the Poor House, later Clifton House, in 1774 that was built by the Belfast Charitable Institute, and for the White Linen Hall in 1783. True to his Episcopalian instincts he built at his own expense a new parish church.

The contrast between the hard-working and prosperous merchant class and the absentee aristocrats was striking. The Presbyterian majority were on the whole much more tolerant than their seventeenth-century forebears. Many believed that prosperity was a sign of divine approval and that it brought responsibility as well as wealth. Most of the town's welfare institutions, amenities and even social life were engendered not by the Donegalls but by the cooperative efforts of the real owners of the town, the factory owners, the merchants, the linen dealers. The commerce that caused Belfast eventually to become one of the leading industrial cities in Britain had had its nucleus from the time of the incorporation of the town in the early seventeenth century. For nearly a hundred years the townsfolk's entrepreneurial skills were not able to achieve much because of lack of real Donegall patronage. Belfast was lucky, however, in that it seemed destined to avoid the unease of the rural province.

As a working eighteenth-century port of emigration, like Derry in the west, it saw many young men and women, mostly younger sons and their wives, leave to try their fortunes in the New World. They became imbued with the ideals of the founding fathers of what was to become the United States and played a significant part when America decided to shake off what they saw as the tyranny of Britain in the War of Independence (1775–82). Benjamin Franklin (1706–90), one of the most brilliant of the founding fathers, estimated that one third of the population of Philadelphia, the country's largest city with 335,000 inhabitants, had been born in Ulster. It was a Maghera man, Charles Thompson (1730–1824), who wrote out in manuscript the actual Declaration of Independence (1776), and it was printed by John Dunlap (1747–1812) who had learned his trade in Strabane. The egalitarian ideals and the notion of entitlement to 'life, liberty and the pursuit of happiness' enshrined in it was communicated to people back in Ireland and had a significant effect in Belfast.

The numbers of Catholics in the town began slowly to grow. They tended to do menial work but they gradually were able to use their skills to improve their situation. There was no Catholic church in the town, the nearest buildings of worship being at Hannahstown and Derriaghy. The penal laws did not formally prevent worship and, as long as priests had no visible signs of their calling, they were largely tolerated. Mass was said on Sundays at Friars Bush in Stranmillis, the site, as the name suggests, of an older Franciscan monastery. The name still persists today in the graveyard behind the Ulster Museum. The few but growing numbers of Catholics were also allowed to attend Mass in a 'waste house' in Castle Street, where the utter lack of amenity meant that worshippers had to bring pieces of wood or bricks to kneel on. It was not until 1783 that St Mary's, a Mass-house, was built in Chapel Lane. Following the cautionary practice elsewhere it was described as a 'chapel', as not having the rooted dignity of a Protestant 'church', suggesting an unthreatening temporariness. Eighty-four pounds, nearly half the cost of the building, were collected from the Protestants of the town, both Anglican and Presbyterian. When the church was ready for occupation, on 30 May 1783, the celebratory mass had in its congregation a company of the Belfast Volunteers in their gorgeous, and often self-designed, dress uniforms. The money was presented to the parish priest, 'the Rev Mr O'Donnell', at the offertory. It was a far cry from the situation of 1708 when one man, Father Phelomy O'Hanlon, had the care of Catholics in Belfast, Derriaghy, Drumbo and Drumbeg. The present day St Mary's Church built on the same site dates from 1868.

The next Catholic church to be built, also with Protestant support, was St Patrick's in Upper Donegall Street, which was opened in 1815. In 1844 a third church, St Malachy's, was built in Alfred Street. By 1861 these were still the only Catholic churches, although the population of that faith, according to the census of that year, was now 41,000.

3

A Radical Town

THE SECOND HALF OF THE EIGHTEENTH century was notably different from the first half with the population increasing from 8,000 in 1757 to 13,000 in 1782. The pattern of town life was already established and the product, which caused the place later to be known as 'Linenopolis', was becoming associated with Belfast throughout western Europe, though the main market for the product was Britain.

One of the main sources of this reputation was Louis Crommelin (1652–1727), a Huguenot born in Picardy who at the age of 33 moved to Amsterdam to escape religious persecution. He came to Lisburn in 1697 at the invitation of William III, bringing with him a band of fellow Huguenots, all skilled in the whole process of linen-making from flax to fabric. The wool industry of Ireland had been deliberately destroyed during the reign of Charles I and this was an attempt at recompense by William.

The most productive area in Ulster was the so-called 'linen triangle', an almost exactly isosceles arrowhead linking Belfast, Armagh and Dungannon. Belfast, because of its position and the entrepreneurial instincts of its citizens, was the centre of the export trade. Soon it began to develop the industrial systems of chemical bleaching and the mechanisation of spinning and weaving. By the

1770s the town was responsible for more than 20 percent of Ireland's linen manufacture and export.

In this process of industrialisation the generally absent Arthur Chichester, now the first Marquis of Donegall (so titled since 1791), took little part. When he did act it was rather in reaction than initiative as when he tried to prevent urban development on the other side of the Long Bridge. Ballymacarrett (or 'Mac Garret's townland') had been bought by the Presbyterian shipper Thomas Pottinger from Lord Clanbrasil in 1672 and he built Mount Pottinger, a suitably grand house for an industrial magnate.[1] His family sold the land to Baron Yelverton in 1779, and Yelverton began to develop the tiny hamlet, which already existed. Donegall regarded that natural development as a threat to his Belfast and he bought it from Yelverton, after some aristocrat persuasion, in 1787. It became an important area of industry with glassworks, a foundry, ropeworks and sheds for linen weaving. The town eventually embraced it in the middle of the next century.

The story of the Chichester family in the nineteenth century is one of disgrace and dissolution. The second marquis, George Augustus, was notorious for his debts that had caused his father great sorrow with Chichester land having to be sold to cover them. After the father's death, and with continually mounting debts, many of them caused by gambling, he was forced to grant land in perpetuity with small rents but at a large initial cost. In this way he disposed of two thirds of his property. Of the 1,520 leases sold, 600 were for Belfast properties. It meant the beginning of the end of their political and social influence but the land seceded enabled the town to grow.

The most significant event of late eighteenth-century Ireland had its source 3,000 miles away. The American Revolutionary War, in which, as we have seen, many Ulster Presbyterians were actively involved, put great strain upon the British standing armies; so many were thought necessary to put manners on the American colonists that Ireland was felt to have been left undefended. The older militias had been disbanded and the vacuum was filled by volunteers, officers from the gentry and aristocracy, and other ranks from the growing numbers of middle classes, both urban and rural.

The Volunteers had never any need to do any fighting but with numbers that rose from 12,000 in the spring of 1779 to 40,000 that September they had become a force of significant political power. The enrolment peaked at 60,000 in 1782, the last year of the American war. Though the Volunteers, especially the upper-class officers, may have looked a little over-gorgeous in their gaudy uniforms they still formed a formidable force. The British government could not help but take their existence seriously and it had to listen when they made a number of demands for reform. Some senior Irish nobles, including the 'Volunteer Earl', James Caulfeild of Charlemont (1728–99), and his adversary, the 'Earl Bishop', Frederick Hervey, 3rd Earl of Bristol (1730–1803), were heavily involved and the Volunteers were able by their efforts to secure the legislative assembly in 1782 that has since become known as 'Grattan's Parliament' after Henry Grattan (1746–1820), its chief minister.

Belfast, with all the energy and constructive envy of what would become later a second city, took to the Volunteers with great enthusiasm. There was opposition from the first marquis but there was little he could do when the early Belfast Company was formed in 1778, appropriately on St Patrick's Day. It was they who imposed upon the movement its military uniforms that became standard countrywide, with heavy 'frogging' on scarlet jackets and a profusion of epaulettes. Though 'patriotic' in the specialised sense used by some members of the Irish Protestant ascendancy who, while remaining loyal to British royalty, would have liked, and for nearly 20 years actually enjoyed, a large amount of legislative and economic independence, few had any concern for the Catholic Irish who formed the greater majority of the country's population. Belfast Volunteers tended to be less instinctively anti-Papist than in other parts of Ulster, especially in north Armagh where Catholics had for 50 years been viewed with extreme suspicion and hatred. According to the letter of the penal laws Catholics could not become members of the Volunteers because they were not allowed to carry arms. Most Ulster companies had few if any Catholics though some were allowed to serve as privates.

It was liberal Belfast who most actively supported the rights of Catholics. On 13 May 1784 the first Belfast Volunteer company passed a resolution to invite to their ranks persons of *every* religious persuasion and were the most insistent about granting full emancipation to the Catholic Irish. By then there were about 1,000 Catholics living in the town, making up a thirteenth of the whole population. This had reached 20,000 by 1800 and by then the town was on the brink of the surge that would make it a leading nineteenth-century industrial city.

The town was still largely Presbyterian with minorities of Episcopalians, Methodists – essentially reformed Episcopalians, followers of John Wesley (1703–91), who visited the town for the second time in 1789 – and Catholics. The Presbyterians were, as ever, industrious, imaginative and liberal in their attitudes. They had created a dynamic town in spite of the aristocratic detachment, not to say neglect, of the Donegalls. They, too, had a kind of schism within their ranks, as conflict between what were called 'New Light' and 'Old Light' clergy increased. The Old Light ministers were Calvinist and intolerant of any deviation from the Westminster Confession; the New Light followers were pragmatic and liberal, and in the ascendant during the latter part of the eighteenth century. By the 1840s the New Light became tainted with the old heresy of Arianism that denied that Christ was co-equal with the Father and was called after its fourth-century originator, Arius of Alexandria (c.250–336). Largely through the efforts of the charismatic and ultra-conservative Henry Cooke (1788–1868), the leading New Light minister Henry Montgomery (1788–1865) was expelled from the assembly in 1840 and for many years thereafter mainstream Presbyterianism was without any trace of liberalism.

The real founders of the town were such people as George

Macartney, who arrived from Scotland in 1640, supplied the area with a clean water supply and became the richest magnate in the town. A descendant of his, Isaac Macartney, built at his own expense two new quays in 1720, which he named the George and the Hanover, a pious recognition of his grandfather and of the new royal house.

Other civic notables were the Englishman, Thomas Waring, who set up the first tannery in the town in 1660 and whose name is remembered in the street by the Custom House in the modern city centre; Robert Joy, who set up the first cotton mill to provide work for the inmates of the Poor House, in a factory conveniently sited in Francis Street, that ran from the aptly named Millfield to Smithfield; and many others, including Nicholas Grimshaw, a cotton printer from Lancashire, who introduced cotton spinning by power at Whitehouse in 1784 on the model of the water-frame and carding machine invented by Sir Richard Arkwright (1732–92) in 1769.

Already the industries for which Belfast would become famous in the nineteenth century – linen and cotton mills, rope and glass manufacture, chemicals and even shipbuilding – were present at least in nucleus. This last industry, still in its infancy, had been begun by an Ayrshire immigrant called William Ritchie (1756–1834). He founded a shipyard on the river at a place used for the export of lime. In 1800 the Ballast Board, the independent body that did most to develop the port, engaged Ritchie to build a proper dry dock. This 'Corporation for Preserving and Improving the Port of Belfast' was given its name from the necessary ballast it provided from dredged material and appropriately it soon removed the shoals that made the docking of ships so difficult, made the use of pilots compulsory, and encouraged Ritchie's enterprises.

There was, however, much more to Belfast than industry. The robust radicalism that was to find its triumph and disaster in the founding of the United Irishmen was already characteristic of the town, showing itself often in its frustrated struggles with the Donegalls. For those who had the means and leisure, the social and intellectual life of the town was rewarding. The Assembly Rooms could be used for refreshments, concerts, recitals, balls, gaming or simple promenading, and they served as a place of social intercourse for the fashionable and pretentious as in a much grander way did the London pleasure gardens of Ranelagh and Vauxhall. In the poem 'Billet to the Company of Players' (1722) by Jonathan Swift (1667–1745), there is a couplet:

> Gallants, next Thursday night will be our last,
> Then without fail, we pack up for Belfast.

It shows that Belfast was clearly on the circuit for travelling companies all through the century. They used what venues were available to them until the erection of such custom-built locations as the Theatre in Mill Gate (near Peter's Hill), which after refurbishment re-opened on 3 April 1770 with *The Suspicious Husband and the Mock Doctor*. This was probably a version by Henry Fielding (1707–54), the author of *Tom Jones* (1749), of Molière's *Le Médecin malgré lui* (1666). Provincial theatres were quick to put on versions of popular successes from Dublin and London, especially since copyright law was so lax. Goldsmith's *She Stoops to Conquer* was presented in Belfast only six months after its London premiere in 1777. Shows of more local interest were also popular. In Derry in 1798 the audiences saw *Just Arrived in L'Derry; or the Thespian from Ennishoen*, while in 1766 the older Belfast theatre, the Vaults, in present day Ann Street, offered *The Humours of Belfast*, a two-act ballad farce, a dramatic form typical of the theatre of the times, of which *The Beggar's Opera* (1728) by John Gay (1685–1732) had the greatest success. Produced by John Rich (1681–1761), the wits of the time observed: 'It made Gay rich and Rich gay.'

During the last 30 years of the century Belfast saw 20 winter seasons in the Mill Gate theatre and in the older one in the Vaults. The great Sarah Siddons (1755–1831), the finest tragic actress of her day, perhaps the greatest Lady Macbeth ever, stunned an elite audience of the town on 6 June 1785 with her performance in *The Unhappy Marriage*. In the audience was Mrs Martha McTier (c.1743–1837), the sister of William Drennan (1754–1820), the main founder of the United Irishmen, and who was married to Samuel, the first president of the Belfast society. She was typical of the educated Belfast women of the period. She was famous as a gambler and for her copious correspondence that has remained a useful archive for historians of the period. She wrote to her brother to advise him that 'five ladies were taken out fainting in the last act, and hardly a man could stand it'.

There are records of five working theatres in the eighteenth-century town. It is not clear when the Vaults, converted from wine stores in Weigh-house Lane, opened but it closed in 1766 because of its lack of proper facilities. The Mill Gate was opened by James Parker on 23 August 1768 but in spite of renovations in 1770 closed eight years later. Like the Vaults it had no boxes and so could not satisfy the first duty of eighteenth-century playgoing: to allow the rich and fashionable to be seen as well as to see. On 23 October 1778 the New Theatre in Ann Street was opened with boxes, a pit and gallery but it proved too small for its eager audiences. Two other theatres were built in the town before the end of the century: one in Rosemary Lane, shockingly near the elegant (and extant) First Presbyterian Church, which raised its curtain first on 3 March 1784 but was found to be structurally unsound; and, finally, on 25 February 1793, a new theatre was launched in Arthur Street. The term 'state of the art' had not been invented then but the latter had many features that the older theatres did not possess: separate doors for box and pit audiences, eight dressing rooms and a large green room.

It was not the most auspicious time to open so volatile an institution as a playhouse in Belfast. The radical views of such townsmen as Drennan, Samuel Neilson (1761–1803), who launched and edited the *Northern Star* (1792–7), the organ of the Ulster United Irishmen, and Henry Joy McCracken (1767–98), who was hanged in the Cornmarket on 17 July 1798, near the tavern in which the United

Irishmen used to meet, and of such temporary residents as Wolfe Tone (1763–98) and Thomas Russell (1767–1803) could lead only to insurgency. The notion of a united body of Irishmen irrespective of class or creed had first been stimulated by the republican ideals of the American colonists who had successfully thrown off British rule and had founded a theoretically democratic country in the United States. Many of the rebels had been born in Ulster, encouraged to independence and egalitarianism by their religion that did not recognise any hierarchical status. The revolution in France, when the Bastille, the empty icon of the *Ancien Régime* fell to cries of '*liberté, égalité, fraternité*' on 14 July 1789, increased the elation of the youngish men who, aflame with a sense of righteousness, wanted an end to monarchy, aristocracy and British influence in Ireland – and an end to discrimination against Catholics.

'Mr Hutton' arrived in Blefuscu on 11 October 1791 to be present at the foundation of the Society of United Irishmen. It was typical of Wolfe Tone's boyishness that he referred to people in his diary with obviously decodable names. *He* was Mr Hutton, the second syllable giving the game away; Blefuscu, the rival island of pygmies to Lilliput in *Gulliver's Travels* (1729), was Belfast, contrasted with the equally minuscule Dublin; his friend from Cork, Thomas Russell, was 'P.P' ('clerk of this parish') and Neilson was dubbed, aptly enough, the 'Jacobin'. His Belfast visit was a mixture of conviviality and seriousness. A typical entry in his journal, that of Sunday, 23 October, includes the admission:

> Went to Donegall Arms and supped on lobsters. Drunk. Very ill-natured to P.P.; P.P. patient. *Mem*: To do so no more.

It is no surprise that the entry for 24 October begins: 'Wakened very sick.' The inauguration took place in Peggy Barclay's tavern in Crown Entry, off High Street, with Samuel McTier in the chair. The society was to be, in Russell's words, 'a union of Irishmen of every religious persuasion in order to obtain a complete reform of the legislature, founded on the principles of civil, political and religious liberty'. Tone was back in Blefuscu in 1792 to celebrate the third anniversary of *Quatorze Juillet* and again in May 1795 when he was en route to exile in America. He noted in his diary:

> I remember particularly two days that we passed on the Cave Hill. On the first Russell, Neilson, Simms [Robert who was a co-founder of the *Northern Star*], McCracken, and one or two more of us, on the summit of McArt's fort took a solemn obligation... never to desist in our efforts until we had subverted the authority of England over our country and asserted her independence.

Those efforts were to be in vain. Most of them died young and violently: McCracken executed after his defeat at Antrim in 1798; Tone later the same year, slowly of septicaemia after a bungled suicide attempt cutting his windpipe but not his jugular ('I'm sorry I have been so bad an anatomist'); Russell hanged in Downpatrick, implicated in the rising of Robert Emmet (1778–1803), and having a posthumous ballad fame as 'The Man from God-Knows-Where', written in 1918 by Florence Mary Wilson (c.1870–1946) from Bangor; Neilson, suddenly, while in exile in Poughkeepsie, New York, in 1803, after giving 'honourable information'. Even Neilson's *Northern Star* perished when the offices and plant were destroyed by the Monaghan militia on 19 May 1797.

The rising, when it came in the summer of 1798, had none of the promised French support in Ulster. An invasion fleet organised by Tone could not land in Bantry Bay in December 1796 because of severe weather, and a further attempt by a Dutch fleet in July 1797 with Tone on board the optimistically named *Vrijheid* ('freedom'), was abandoned because of storms. When it sailed three weeks later without Tone it was annihilated by the English fleet under Admiral Adam Duncan (1731–1804) off the north Dutch village of Camperdown.

The reactions of the populace of Belfast were mixed; the small number of republicans (or democrats, as they liked to call themselves) grieved that their best hope of a successful revolution had gone. The part-time soldiers of the largely Catholic militias and the entirely Protestant Yeomanry would have been no match for the highly trained troops of the Revolution. Other citizens, a majority, held a meeting at the end of 1797 to raise money for the widows and orphans of the British sailors who died at Camperdown. McCracken, not long released from imprisonment in Dublin, remained true to the revolutionary ideals. He led 4,000 men to capture Randalstown and Ballymena on 6 June 1798. He was defeated the next day at Antrim by Colonel Durham. He hid out for a time in the hill country at Slemish near Ballymena and later in Colin Glen and Cave Hill while his sister Mary Ann tried to arrange a passage to America. He was betrayed, as were so many other United Irishmen, and arrested by the Carrickfergus militia. Another outbreak in County Down on 9 June led by the Lisburn draper, Henry Munro (1758–98), lasted four days until his defeat by General George Nugent on the thirteenth. He was hanged opposite his own house on 15 June.

The insurrection in Ulster (and other places) was essentially defeated two years before it began. The policy of frightfulness adopted by General Gerard Lake (1744–1808) with the use of the remobilised militias (mainly Catholic with Protestant officers) and the new Yeomanry (largely members of the Orange Order that had been founded in County Armagh in 1795) proved to be very effective. A kind of martial law was declared with Habeas Corpus suspended and floggings and burnings the rule. Belfast was understood correctly to be the source of disaffection. In 1797 Lake wrote to Thomas Pelham, the chief secretary, observing that, 'every act of sedition originates in this town… Nothing but terror will keep them in order.'

Terror *did* keep them in order. The houses of known republicans were attacked and some were publicly flogged. The destruction of the offices of the *Northern Star* was part of that terror campaign. It was ironic that the official troops used in this 'cleansing' were largely Catholic militiamen and that their quarry were Protestant republicans.

Lake's announcement of martial law was published in the *Belfast News Letter* on 13 March 1797 and offered rewards to those who gave information as to where 'illegal Arms and Ammunition' might be seized. Most of the informal soldiery were disarmed with the notable exception of the Orange Yeomanry. The leaders – Neilson, Russell and McCracken – had been arrested and spent time in Kilmainham Jail between 1796 and 1797. Neilson and McCracken were released but Russell was kept in prison until 1798, before being sent to join other '98 leaders in Fort George on the Moray Firth in Scotland. He was released from this not unpleasant incarceration a year before his death in 1803.

During the troubled summer of 1798 Belfast was quiet. There was a blanket near-curfew imposed by a strong Yeoman presence. Each house had to display a notice indicating a list of its inhabitants. Within a year it was almost as if the heady days of republican fervour had never existed. Early in 1798, Thomas Percy (1729–1811), the Anglican Bishop of Dromore and compiler of the famous *Reliques of Ancient English Poetry* (1765), noticed a change in the political climate. He wrote to his wife:

> A wonderful change has taken place among republicans in the north, especially in or near Belfast… They now abhor the French as much as they were formerly partial to them.

This echoes Mrs McTier's remarks in a letter to her brother, when news of the Terror reached Ireland:

> I am turned, quite turned against the French, & fear that it is all farther than ever from coming to good.

Drennan himself was shocked by the news from Paris and the realisation of what bloody revolution usually entailed cooled his own ardour. Though one of the society of United Irishmen's founders, he realised he had no stomach for violence. He remained, however, a dedicated radical and a vocal campaigner for Catholic Emancipation.

The business instinct of Belfast townspeople was equally as strong as that of radicalism, and even enthusiastic United Irishmen like William Drennan preferred business. After his acquittal for sedition in 1794 he withdrew from active participation in the society's activities. Robert Simms, who was active in the running of the *Northern Star*, resigned in the spring of 1798. The respect that Belfast people showed to commerce had already been noticed by visitors. Jacques Louis de Bougrenet, Chevalier de La Tocnaye, a fugitive from the Terror, walked round Ireland and recorded his impressions in *Promenade d'un français dans l'Irlande* (1798). In Belfast in 1797 he noted:

> Belfast has almost entirely the look of a Scotch town, and the character of the inhabitants has considerable resemblance to that of the people of Glasgow. If you start a conversation with them about the Emperor or General Clairfaix, they will possibly talk about the prices of sugar and linen, according as they are trading in one or the other, and may remark that if peace is not made promptly they do not know how they are going to get rid of their muslin or how they are to buy wine.

By 1800 the rising was no longer talked about; political conversations were now all about the proposed Act of Union which William Pitt (1759–1806) intended to impose by any means, fair or foul, as the answer to the Irish question, with the offer of total Catholic Emancipation to please the Papists. The promise of emancipation meant, ironically, that the Orange Order fought against it during the murky dealings that led to the Irish parliament voting itself out of existence. The bribery that eased its demise was typical of the period and the misguided Catholic support was useful to the passing of the act that became law on 1 January 1801. The Orange Order need not have concerned itself with the possible amelioration of Papists. George III (1738–1820), showing a surprisingly pious adherence to his coronation oath, refused to allow any further concessions to Catholics. Pitt, of course, resigned the premiership but felt it his duty to return to office in 1804 because of the incompetence of his successor and the renewed war with Napoleon. The very title, 'United Kingdom of Great Britain and Ireland', gave the game away that it had been a misalliance, if not an actual shotgun wedding.

The nature of the country changed with the flight of the later earls. Many of the Irish aristocracy, finding life in Britain more congenial, left and the elegant eighteenth-century capital became a dusty provincial city. This degradation had been anticipated by 'Pleasant Ned' Lysaght (1763–1810), one of the Dublin wits who fought against the act. In his poem 'A Prospect' (1800), he wrote:

> Thro' Capel Street as you rurally range,
> You'll scarcely recognise it the same street;
> Choice turnips shall grow in your Royal Exchange
> And fine cabbages down along Dame Street.
> …
> Our Custom House quay, full of weeds, of rare sport,
> But the Ministers' minions, kind elves, sir!
> Will give free leave all our goods to export
> When we've got none at home for ourselves, sir!

Belfast, fortunate as ever, actually benefited from the legislation. A few decades into the new century it was clear that the old radical flame was all but extinguished. Belfast was a safe Unionist Protestant town and one that Westminster could judiciously favour. The next hundred years saw the development of the city – chartered in 1888 – into one of the largest and most productive industrial centres in what was then unselfconsciously called the British Isles.

4

'The Athens of the North'

THIS COMPLIMENTARY TITLE WAS APPLIED FIRST to Edinburgh partly because of a fancied physical resemblance to the Greek capital – it had a kind of acropolis in the castle and its volcanic rock – and partly because of the unfinished ornamental classical buildings on Calton Hill that used to be known as the 'disgrace of Edinburgh'. Belfast took the title by force and applied it to the late eighteenth-century town, at first because of its tradition of democracy, regarded as Athens's invention, and also because of the founding of such institutions as the Belfast Reading Society (1788), which became the Belfast Library and Society for Promoting Knowledge, the Belfast Academical Institution (1814), and the Belfast Natural History and Philosophical Society (1821). Charles Montieth, the publisher, who was a pupil at 'Inst', the school that grew out of the Academical Institution, once asked a teacher if Belfast was actually known as the 'Athens of the North'. The teacher replied: 'I'm pretty sure you are right but of one thing I'm absolutely certain: Athens was never known as the "Belfast of the South"!'

The Reading Society and its later incarnation, the Belfast Library, had its collection of volumes stored at first in such hostelries as Ireland's, Drew's, and the Donegall Arms in Castle Place, where the members used to meet. This practice was obviously unsuitable, especially as the greater majority of members were Presbyterian. Robert Cary, a founder member, offered a room in his own house to act as meeting place, book deposit and store of artefacts that formed the nucleus of a town museum.

The founder members were in the words of the indefatigable Martha McTier, 'worthy plebians [sic] who would do honour to any town… not among them one of the higher rank McCormick the gunsmith or Osborne the baker'. Soon they were joined by members of the professional and merchant classes, including the rich Waddell Cunningham, who dared to challenge the Donegall elite; Nicholas Grimshaw, the cotton manufacturer; Dr William Bruce, minister of the Rosemary Lane Presbyterian Church and principal of the Belfast Academy (founded in 1786), whom Tone described unjustly, in his anticlerical way, as an 'intolerant high priest'; and Fr Hugh O'Donnell, parish priest of the recently built church in Chapel Lane. Only in egalitarian Belfast could the classes have mixed so companionably.

Cary emigrated to America in 1794 and the library and museum, under its new librarian, Thomas Russell, moved to a house in Ann Street. The society found a home eventually in the White Linen Hall, the elegant complex, designed by Roger Mulholland, the carpenter with architectural genius who was personally responsible for most of the finest buildings in Georgian Belfast, including the Rosemary Lane Presbyterian Church. The proprietors offered 'to the society the Room over the central part of the Linen Hall for the library free of all expense'. The Linen Hall was to be the home of the worthy Belfast library from 1802 until it moved a little distance away to the former linen warehouse of Moore & Weinberg in Donegall Square North. For many reasons, including the sentimental, it retained and still proudly maintains the old name.

Another famous Belfast institution (in several senses) that dates from the 'Athenian' period is 'Inst'. It and the earlier Belfast Academy had been founded to provide a kind of combined secondary- and third-level education that was closed to Presbyterians in Ireland and one that would be considerably less expensive and troublesome than crossing to Glasgow or Edinburgh. It was founded as the Belfast Academical Institution in 1810 by Drennan and his colleague John Templeton (1766–1825) and though non-denominational became in effect a Presbyterian seminary until the Arian controversy of 1830 when such anti-New Light polemicists as Henry Cooke accused many of the staff of heresy. William IV allowed 'Royal' to be added to the title in 1831. The opening of the Queen's College in 1845 and the neighbouring Assembly's College four years later removed the need for a third-level curriculum.

The Queen's Colleges in Belfast, Cork and Galway, established by Sir Robert Peel (1788–1850) in his attempt to diminish support for the repeal of the Act of Union, were declared 'godless' by orthodox Presbyterians and the Catholic hierarchy because of their secular standing. This led to the building of Assembly's College suspiciously close to the Queen's campus in Belfast and the establishment in Dublin in 1854 of the Catholic University, with John Henry Newman (1801–90) as its first rector.

Inst, as it has become universally known, reverted to being a boys' secondary school, one of the best known in Ireland. The son of its professor of mathematics was William Thomson, later Lord Kelvin (1824–1907), who proposed the SI unit of temperature and had the honour of having it called after his peerage name, from the stream that flows past Glasgow University, where he was professor of natural philosophy for 53 years.[1] When he retired in 1899 he was entitled to write after his name more academic honours than any man alive. Some of these may be read on the plinth of his statue at the entrance to Botanic Gardens Park.

One of the interesting and eventually significant initiatives of the Belfast Library and Society for Promoting Knowledge was the organising in 1792 of the Belfast Harp Festival in the Assembly Rooms of the Exchange, one of the visible contributions made by the

Donegalls to the social and cultural life of the town. The chief promoters were the surgeon James McDonnell (1763–1845), founder of the old Royal Hospital in Frederick Street, Robert Simms of the *Northern Star*, and Henry Joy (1754–1835), editor of the *Belfast News Letter* and grandson of its founder. The McCracken siblings, Henry Joy and Mary Ann (1770–1866), were also involved, the practical sister prevailing upon their young lodger, the Armagh-born Edward Bunting (1773–1843), the under-organist at St Anne's parish church since 1784, to come along. It was the first of many useful things that eminent philanthropist would do for her native town. Robert Bradshaw, the secretary and treasurer of the committee, placed an advertisement in the *News Letter* on 26 April requesting 'PERFORMERS ON THE IRISH HARP… to assemble in this town on the 10th day of July next when a considerable sum will be distributed in premiums in proportion to their merit.' An earlier notice had promised 'a subscription' which the committee intended 'to apply in attempting to revive and perpetuate the Ancient music and Poetry of Ireland'.

These notices also appeared in newspapers in Waterford, Kilkenny, Galway, Sligo and Derry and, in all, ten Irish *cruitirí* and one Welshman made their way to Belfast. Six of them were blind and the youngest was 15. One of the more colourful characters was the blind Denis Hempson – or O'Hempsey (1695–1807) – who, at 97, was the oldest contributor. He had played for Bonnie Prince Charlie at Holyrood Palace during his attempt on the British throne in 1745. Born in Garvagh, County Derry, he was given a house in Magilligan by the Earl-Bishop, married at 86 and sired a daughter. He was the last performer to play *ar an sean-nós* ('in the traditional way') with long, carefully hooked fingernails.

The first prize was won by Charles Fanning from Cavan, the second by the blind Art Ó Néill from Tyrone, who had been McDonnell's tutor. Rose Mooney, the only woman, got third prize. All the players were given money and the three-day event stunned fashionable Belfast;

the diligent Martha McTier wrote to her brother to say that the Irish music was 'all the rage'. One distinguished visitor was underwhelmed: 'Mr Hutton' wrote in his dairy in his usual trenchant way:

> July 11th: All go to the Harpers at one; poor enough; ten performers; seven execrable, three good, one of them, Fanning, far the best. No new musical discovery; believe all the good Irish airs are already written…
> July 13th: The Harpers again. Strum. Strum and be hanged.

Tone was no better a musicologist than an anatomist. What he did not realise was that the strummers were the custodians of a wealth of music that might have well perished with them.

The Harp Festival was a glowing social success but it lasted a mere three days. Mary Ann McCracken's insistence that her young friend Bunting should act as a kind of scribe, assiduously writing down the tunes that he listened to in the heat of the Assembly Rooms was the lasting result of the gathering. He became an enthusiastic collector of the extant tunes, travelling all over the country with pen and manuscript paper. This energy was uncharacteristic; Bunting was really rather lazy. *A General Collection of the Ancient Irish Music* that contained 66 airs was not published until 1796 but it had saved a vanishing treasure. The money spent by the Society on its publication was more than recouped within five years. Other collections followed with proximate titles, each containing the words 'Ancient Music of Ireland', in 1809 and 1840. Tom Moore (1779–1852) used airs from the first collection as settings for his song lyrics that became famous as the *Irish Melodies* (1807–1834).

On Bunting's foray into Connacht and other parts in search of old airs he was accompanied by an Irish scholar, Patrick Lynch (aka Pádraic Ó Loinsigh), from Loughinisland, who taught Irish in the Belfast Academy and gave private lessons to McDonnell and Thomas Russell. He transcribed the Irish words of the native speakers and made translations of them. Bunting remained intensely apolitical in spite of his close friendship with the McCrackens and did not use Lynch again because of the latter's friendship with and involvement in the trial of Russell in 1803. A portly, easygoing bachelor, Bunting finally married, in 1819, a Miss Chapman and moved to Dublin. The ancient music of Ireland had made him famous but, as Martha McTier made known, 'Sugar plumbs or sweetys is his greatest temptation, for he despises both money and praise.' During his sojourn as musical director of the Belfast Harp Festival (1803–13) he conducted in the Second Presbyterian Church the first local performance of Handel's *Messiah*.

Both Bunting and Sir John Stevenson (c.1760–1833), Moore's arranger, have been accused of making lush concert arrangements of the original pure Irish tunes and Bunting ignored Lynch's versions of the original words and commissioned other versifiers to fit 'suitable' words to 'his' tunes. Moore's use of the tunes from Bunting's first volume, Bunting described as theft, as if his transcriptions conferred copyright. The arrangements that the purists objected to were what endeared the melodies to the Regency drawing rooms and gave the Minstrel Boy a career and an entrée into polite society.

Patrick Lynch continued to play an important part in the preservation of the Irish language in east Ulster. There were still native speakers in parts of the Antrim glens and in Tyrone and south Armagh. In an essay called 'Our National Language', printed in the *Nation* (1842–8), the newspaper that he founded with Charles Gavan Duffy (1816–1903) and John Blake Dillon (1816–66), Thomas Davis (1814–45) had a typically pragmatic approach. The paper was essentially a weekly compendium of adult education for the growing nationalist population and Davis's enthusiasm was powerful and his logic inexorable. His argument for the use of Irish was put very strongly: 'To lose your native language and learn that of an alien is the worst badge of conquest.' But his innate practicality marches side by side with the rhetoric. Irish was not dead; at the time of writing in 1844, '...half the people west of a line from Derry to Waterford [almost exactly north–south] speak Irish habitually and in some of the mountain tracts east of that line it is still common'.

Aware of linguistic erosion, a number of concerned scholars and laymen had tried a number of revival initiatives. One of the most successful was the Society for the Preservation of the Irish Language (SPIL), established in 1887 by Clareman David Comyn (1854–1907), a clerk in the Dublin National Bank founded by the 'Liberator', Daniel O'Connell (1775–1847).[2] Their publication *Irisleabhar na Gaedhilge* ('The Gaelic Journal') acted as a preservative and enabled the great surge in recovery that was generated by the Gaelic League after its foundation on 31 July 1893. One notable success of SPIL was the acceptance of Irish as a subject for the new Intermediate Certificate examination. It was achieved by wearisome lobbying and the calling of the subject 'Celtic'.

Belfast's awareness of the language was stimulated by the enthusiasm generated by the Harp Festival. In 1795 Patrick Lynch's compendium *Bolg anTsolar* [recte *Bolg an tSoláthair*] – literally translated as 'the belly of the provision' and used to signify the word 'magazine' – was published by the *Northern Star* for 13 pence. It was a small volume, duodecimo in format (the smallest size got by folding the standard printing sheet to make twelve leaves) and 180 pages long. *The Gaelic Magazine,* as it was known in English, was an interesting publication. There were poems and songs and a translation by the recently deceased Charlotte Brooke (c.1740–93), the Cavan scholar, of a tale of the Fianna. There was also a short Irish grammar, a vocabulary and useful Irish phrases. It was the only number published because two years later, as we have seen, the paper's offices were wrecked by the Monaghan militia. It was, however, reissued in 1837 with a cover showing a crown and a harp, and the words *Éirinn go bráth* ('Ireland forever') written at the bottom. That motto was to appear frequently on banners, flags and collarettes in Irish communities in England, America and Australia after the great diaspora of the mid-century Famine.

The reissue was arranged by one of Belfast's most prodigious Gaelic enthusiasts, Robert Shipboy McAdam (1808–95) – or Roibeard Mac

Ádaimh, as he preferred to be known. Typically, considering the town's character and history, he was an industrialist and a Presbyterian. He and his brother James (1801–61), another amateur with a strong interest in geology, and first librarian of the Queen's College, could indulge their penchant for scholarship because of the Soho Engineering Foundry that they established in Townsend Street between the Lower Falls and Shankill in 1832. Both were educated at Inst and deeply interested in things Gaelic. The Ulster Gaelic Society – *Cuideacht Gaedhilge Uladh* – founded by Robert in 1838 was almost certainly the first language revival initiative in Ireland. Its purposes were 'the preservation of the remains of Irish literature, maintaining teachers of the Irish language and publishing useful books in that language'. Irish had been available in Inst since 1818 when it was known as the Belfast Academical Institution and continued to be taught there intermittently until the founding of Queen's College in 1849. In 1852 John O'Donovan (1806–61), who had worked for the Ordnance Survey on Irish placenames, was appointed to the chair of Celtic Studies and, though he had no students, gave annual lectures.

McAdam's determination to keep the flame of Irish alive led him to invite to the town Aodh Mac Domhnaill (1802–67), a native speaker from County Meath. As Cathal O'Byrne (1874–1957), Belfast's most famous antiquary, records in his book *As I Roved Out* (1946), he was set up in 88 Millfield – a house now gone – by McAdam as a 'teacher of Irish' and a 'Gaelic scribe', transcribing Irish manuscripts. His title 'the Belfast poet' was challenged by Art Mac Bionaid (1793–1879) from south Armagh, another poet and scholar, who questioned his competence in a splendidly vicious piece of satirical verse, '*D'imigh an t-iasc a bhí san Bhóinn*' ('The fish that was in the Boyne has gone'). In it, all the fauna of Ireland and even the very towns are said to be agitated at the prospect of Mac Domhnaill being regarded as a true poet. They were reconciled when Mac Domhnaill wrote a poem, '*Nach tursach mo thuras an tráth so*', describing the actual miseries of his working life:

Nach tursach mo thuras an tráth so, ag pilleadh ó chlár na Midhe
Gan duine mo chuideacht san lá nó cumann le mná san oídhch'…
('This journey from Meath's plain – O what a plight!
With no man's company by day nor woman's at night.')

'*Aodh Gaedalach*' ('Hugh the Gael'), as he called himself, made
one lasting contribution to his adopted town, the poem '*I mBéul Áth
Fearsde chois Chuain*'. In it he celebrates two other Irish scholars
and scribes, Larry Duff and the ex-army surgeon, Samuel Bryson:

I mBéul Áth Fearsde chois cuain ag bruach na fairrge
Tá beirt dhaoine uaisle tá stuama meanmnach…
('In Belfast by the bay on the edge of the sea
Are two cheery gentlemen, wise as can be…')

McAdam continued to work for the preservation of the residual
Irish culture and the development of the aesthetic life of his town.
He was one of the founders of the *Ulster Journal of Archaeology* in
1853 and was of course heavily involved in the other societies that
perhaps allowed the town to claim some 'Athenian' dimension. As
well as the library, the harp and literary societies, there were two
other cultural agencies: the Belfast Natural History and Philosophical
Society and the Belfast Naturalists' Field Club. The first of these,
founded in 1821, had collected enough material to establish a museum
ten years later in College Square, still remembered in the name the
Old Museum Building, now an arts centre. Its contents were presented
to the city in 1910 and form the basis of the Ulster Museum in
Botanic Gardens Park. The second of these was founded in 1863,
the first of its kind in Ireland. The regular surveys organised by the
club yielded valuable information about local flora and fauna that is
useful even today.

In 1833 William Crolly (1780–1849), the Bishop of Down and
Connor, following the obligation imposed upon him by the Council
of Trent (1545–63) to provide a junior diocesan seminary for the
education of priests, established St Malachy's College at the foot of
the Antrim Road near Carlisle Circus. Ireland's turbulent history in

the intervening three hundred years, including the period of Cromwellian savagery and the Popery Laws of Queen Anne, precluded the implementation of the council's diktat. Now in the times of relative peace the ideal of a junior seminary was achieved. Not all the students, of course, were considering the priesthood as a career but the school curriculum, with its greater emphasis on religion and ancient classics than on science, was also considered appropriate for the sons of the growing numbers of bourgeois Catholics. The ideal that the founders of Inst hoped for of having a non-denominational school system was not to be achieved. Sectarianism had not yet become the most obvious characteristic of the town, largely because of the relatively small Catholic population, at just 20,000 about a third of the population, but its seeds had been sown.

The system of 'national schools' in operation since 1831 had been the government's response to the charge that primary schools largely funded by proselytising Protestant societies were unacceptable to Catholics. It took several decades before the hierarchy obtained what they considered a sufficient control over the curriculum. Most of the crusade in Belfast had been begun by Patrick Dorrian (1814–85), Bishop of Down and Connor from 1865, who greatly strengthened church structures in Belfast. Unlike Cornelius Denvir, his predecessor, who had preferred accommodation with the existing system with reasonable safeguards, Dorrian, like most post-Famine clerics, inspired by Paul Cullen (1803–78), the archbishop of Armagh and later Dublin, sought discipline and even obedience from his steadily growing flock. He and his immediate successors established a Catholic town that lived uneasily within the larger urban boundaries with a culture that persisted until the coming of the Troubles of the 1970s. He built many Catholic primary schools, obtained land for a Catholic cemetery in Milltown in 1870 and an industrial school for boys in the same district. One of his earliest educational initiatives was the bringing of members of the Irish Christian Brothers to help with the primary education of boys. They set up primary schools in Divis Street (1866),

Donegall Street (1867), and Oxford Street (1874), the last specifically for dockland children, as suggested by the philanthropic McGill family who subsidised the cost of building. A technical school, or trade school, as it was called at the time, was opened in 1903 in Hardinge Street, a thoroughfare that has since disappeared. It ran parallel to the New Lodge Road down to North Queen Street.

The Brothers' schools were very popular with parents if not the pupils and highly successful. Their secondary school set up soon afterwards began to rival Dorrian's own diocesan St Malachy's and there was a period of conflict between order and ordinary until the Brothers were permitted in 1879 to enter their pupils for the public examinations and let the school become what it has remained – now in Glen Road – an alternative grammar school. Other teaching orders that played their part in the education of the city children were the Sisters of Mercy and the de La Salle Brothers. Bishop Dorrian also founded the hospital run by the Sisters of Mercy, later known as the Mater Infirmorum in the Crumlin Road.

The pioneer of girls' education in the town was Margaret Moore (1832–1912) from Rathfriland. She was a missionary widow whose husband, the Rev John Byers, had died in Shanghai when she was just 21, and the mother of a baby. Well-educated herself at a progressive school in Nottingham she set up the Ladies Collegiate at 13 Wellington Place in 1859. Mrs Byers' school moved to Howard Street, the Dublin Road, and finally settled at Lower Crescent, between Botanic Avenue and University Road, in 1873. It was to remain there for nearly a hundred years. It became Victoria College in 1870 when the queen herself graciously granted the royal title. A plaque on the wall of the Crescent Arts Centre commemorates its long-term location and the name of its charismatic founder.

The old radicals might have disapproved of a school for females only. Girls as well as boys (including Mary Ann McCracken) had attended the school in High Street set up by the enlightened educationalist, David Manson, in 1760. Victorian Belfast, however, was notably different from the egalitarian town of the earlier century. Nineteenth-century decorum had replaced the freer mores of the eighteenth. Secondary education for Catholic girls was begun in 1870 with the opening of St Dominic's High School on the Falls Road.

The 'godless' Queen's College, apart from its importance as an institution of third-level education, had the side effect of changing the nature of two ambivalent foundations. Inst no longer straddled second and third level but became a leading grammar school for boys. Its association with the internal struggles of Presbyterianism ceased with the building of a seminary for postulant divines that became known as Assembly's College, and has continued to be called that. It was regarded as free from the taint of Arianism that was supposed to be endemic in Inst.

Belfast was not designated a city until 1888, a fact occasionally remarked upon by the second Ulster city – Derry – which had had the status since 1613. By then other creeds had established their own confessional institutions. The Wesleyan Methodist Collegiate institution was set up in 1868 across the road from the Queen's College and admitted 'young ladies' from its fourth month of existence. It became known as Methodist College in 1885 but has been known affectionately since as Methody. One wing of the original college served as a theological seminary that moved in 1918 to separate premises called 'Edgehill' in Lennoxvale, about half a mile away; this became Edgehill College ten years later and in 1951 became a constituent college of the Queen's University of Belfast. Methody in its original Malone Road site and Inst in College Square, to which it gave the name, remain two of Ireland's finest grammar schools.

Belfast's oldest surviving school was founded as the Belfast Academy in 1786 by the merchants of the Presbyterian town as a place 'in which the sons of gentlemen who could not conveniently be sent to college might receive a liberal education'. Its first site was in present-day Academy Street, by St Anne's cathedral. Like Inst, its friendly rival, it too was intended to have third-level elements. It moved to its present site in Cliftonville Road in 1880 and was granted the right to call itself Belfast Royal Academy by Queen Victoria (1819–1902) in 1888.

In 1894 Belfast got Campbell College, its first boys' boarding school, that aimed to emulate the ideal of the English public school. St Malachy's had, of course, had boarders since its inception in 1833 but now Henry James Campbell, a wealthy linen merchant, provided the money to build the school at Belmont, near the parkland that was to be the site of the parliament building of Stormont.

The growing prosperity of the town was reflected in the number of impressive buildings that graced it. None had the simple Georgian elegance of the White Linen Hall, the Academical Institute – designed by Sir John Soane (1753–1837), the leading English architect of the time – or Clifton House, but Queen's College (1846), in its neo-Tudor red brick (Victorian Belfast's favourite building material), seemed to suit the place's self-perception. It was the work of Charles Lanyon (1813–88), who was also responsible for the Queen's Bridge (1845), the prison (1846) and courthouse (1850) in the Crumlin Road, Assembly's College (1853), and the Custom House (1857). He was also responsible for the design of the remarkable coast road that runs from Larne to Portrush, which had the effect of opening up the famous Nine Glens and gave them previously unavailable access to the sea. A civil engineer by training, it was a natural instinct that he should work on the new railroads, designing the line from Belfast to Ballymena, and engineering the vital Belfast–Holywood–Bangor railway link.

Lanyon and his partners – William Henry Lynn and his son John Lanyon – were essentially the creators of the public buildings of Belfast. As well as the imposing edifices already named the firm was responsible for the Public Library in Royal Avenue, the Methodist Memorial Church at Carlisle Circus and the modern Belfast Castle, which was commissioned by the Donegalls and completed in the fashionable Scottish-Baronial style in 1867. The age of Georgian simplicity had gone and now the heavier and more ornate Victorian style of public building was beginning to replace it.

The Lanyon partnership's main rival in nineteenth-century Belfast was the short-lived WJ Barre (1830–67) who came from Newry to work in the big town. The reputation of Lanyon was such that though Barre's designs for the building of Scrabo Tower had won first place, the Lanyon firm got the job. The same bullying trick was tried when Barre's designs were chosen for the new Albert Clock but Lanyon was awarded the contract. Barre made it known publicly that Lanyon was a member of the selection committee and in the ensuing scandal he was given the job. As well as the striking monument to the Prince Consort, completed in 1867, Barre was also responsible for the Ulster Hall (1860), then and for many years the largest public hall in the town.

One of the more glaring examples of architectural intrusion is the masking of part of the façade of Inst by the bulky building of the College of Technology, which looks like a close relation of the more opulent City Hall but had a different architect, Samuel Stevenson, and dates from 1902. To add to the insult, it was built on land that Inst was forced to sell. The greatest architectural crime of the century, however, according to purists, was the demolition of the White Linen Hall to provide a site for the new City Hall. Strictly speaking it was Edwardian rather than Victorian. The architect was a 30-year-old Englishman called Brumwell Thomas and his design has been compared to an over-elaborate wedding cake. It was, however, what prosperous Belfast demanded for the first decade of the twentieth century. It was completed in 1906 and is now so much the visual identifier of the city that it is impossible to think that it is only a hundred years old.

Other buildings were less grand and not so respectable. Theatre had suffered in the middle years of the nineteenth century from the reputation of its houses. Attendance at the theatre was regarded at best as an unnecessary and unprofitable waste of time, at worst as morally deleterious. The clergy of all denominations were conscious of a steadily growing population about whose moral welfare they had the greatest fears. These new citizens inevitably were mainly rural and unaccustomed to the straitness of town life. They were mainly poor and in the prevailing industrial culture extremely hard-working. In their sparse hours of leisure they did not look either for subtlety or elegance. They needed liquor and music-hall entertainment, preferably provided by the same building. These would, as we shall see, be supplied. Entrepreneurial instinct, with its acute perception of what the public wants, can often override the prevailing bourgeois morality.

5

Cotton, Linen, Rope and Ships

THE CONFIDENT EDWARDIAN CITY HAD VISIBLE evidence of success in its opulent City Hall, its impressive department store Robinson and Cleaver (1888) – the same age as the city – and even more iconic, across the street in Donegall Square East, the Scottish Providential Institution, the friezes of which celebrated in stone the chief elements of the city's industrial greatness: textiles, shipbuilding and ropeworks. Things had changed since the lively, lately radical town marked the Act of Union in 1801. The population, 8,549 in 1757, had increased to 18,320 in 1791. By 1841 it was 75,308 but by 1901, when Belfast had become one of the leading industrial cities in Europe, it was nearly five times as large with a population of 349,180.

Cotton was the first commodity to exercise the talent of the town's industrialists. Cotton manufacture was first considered as an appropriate occupation for the orphans who inhabited the elegant Georgian Poorhouse (now Clifton House) though it is unlikely that its inmates appreciated its architectural elegance. This benevolence ceased with the realisation that with water-power, supplied by the fast streams that ran off the Antrim hills, cotton manufacture could be mechanised. As local manufacturers became aware of industrial developments in the Lancashire cotton towns they began to use steam power instead. By 1820 there were 15 cotton mills in or near the town, employing 2,000 hands. 'King cotton' had a relatively short reign because the Belfast manufacturers realised that the textile for which the town would become famous throughout the world was more profitable: Belfast was on the way to becoming 'Linenopolis'.

Again it was developments in Britain that spurred some of the Belfast cotton manufacturers to change. James Kay, a Leeds inventor, had discovered a means of producing linen yarn by a wet spinning process. The alert Belfast businessmen were kept aware of these and other industrial advances and it was the burning down of the cotton mill that Thomas Mulholland (1786–1830) had built in Henry Street, off York Street, in 1828, that proved to be a spur to linen manufacture in the town.

The textile had had its place in the town's commerce for many years but it acted largely as a marketing and export centre for the cottage industries of the 'linen triangle'. Now with cotton spinning beginning to decline slightly Mulholland and his brothers Andrew (1790–1866) and St Clair (1798–1872) decided to modify their mills in Winetavern Street, off North Street, and Francis Street close by. They visited Leeds, York and Lancaster in the company of John Hind, a linen expert from Ballynure, and on their return set up 1,000 flax spinners in Francis Street. The York Street mill was rebuilt in 1830, the year of Thomas's death, and its 8,000 spindles made Andrew extremely rich and caused many of the other cotton manufacturers to change to linen.

Andrew became mayor of the town in 1845, the first year of the Great Famine. This calamity thwarted his ambitious philanthropic plans for the town, which had included the provision of public gardens, wash-houses and free libraries but he did make a great deal of money available to relieve the hunger and disease among the many refugees who had flocked to the town when the potato crops continued to fail. His lasting material contribution to Belfast was the provision in 1862 of the great organ in the Ulster Hall. St Clair

Mulholland and Hind became partners and their mill in Durham Street became the biggest in the town, employing 800 people.

According to the trade directory for 1831 Andrew Mulholland's was the only linen mill in Belfast, but by 1835 there were a dozen flax-spinning factories in the steadily growing town. That number had risen to 32 by 1860, while there were only two mills still spinning cotton. Belfast was spared the slump that afflicted the Lancashire millers when the American Civil War (1861–5) cut off supplies of raw cotton from the United States. The linen industry could hardly escape the boom that followed, now that it was possible to weave the finer linen using power looms. By 1861 there were nearly 5,000 of these machines operating in Linenopolis and the boom in sales continued all during the American war. Between 1867 and 1870 there was a severe slump partly caused by a resurgence of cotton supplies but when it ended Belfast, now the largest producer of linen in the world, was able to recover its wealth. It had then 15,000 looms in full production making cambrics, damasks and diapers (used mainly for table linen). The industry produced a characteristic female worker as identifiable in working-class women as shipyard workers in men. Until the industry declined with the surge in the availability of man-made fibres after the Second World War they provided the world, especially America, with the other eminently desirable Irish artefact to match Waterford crystal.

Belfast was the only Irish industrial city, the equivalent of Manchester, Birmingham and the conglomerate of small towns that made up the Black Country of the north midlands. Its factory owners had the same attitude to their operatives as any Lancashire cotton magnate or Bradford wool millionaire. The crusade for the amelioration of working conditions by Anthony Ashley Cooper, 7th Earl of Shaftesbury (1801–85), that led to the Factory Acts (1833–50) had eventually some success in lessening the number of hours that women and children were allowed to work (and thus effectively men) but for many years the masters tried to circumvent the regulations. It was not that they were all flint-hearted Bounderbys but rather that they were devout subscribers to the doctrine of *laissez-faire*, an inexorable law of economics that did not permit intervention in the relations between master and man. Health and safety matters were hardly considered and the linen mills were both actively and passively dangerous. Regulations that demanded safety guards for machines were usually ignored and it proved almost impossible for factory inspectors to secure convictions right to the end of the century.

The air in the mills was full of tiny particles, as lethal as asbestos fibre, which caused bronchial and gastric illness, and led to a life expectancy of just 45 years. Carding, done mainly by women, was even more injurious to health. It led to uncontrollable fits of coughing and spitting blood, all this during a working day that began at 5am and lasted with only two half-hour breaks until 7 or 8pm. The most dangerous place in the mill was the preparing room where the textile dust was so fine that one supervisor called it 'slow death'. 'Phthisis' (the nineteenth-century medical term for tuberculosis) was common. Women were the preferred workforce since their pay was small compared to that of men. They usually worked barefoot and onychia, the inflammation of the nail bed, an extremely painful condition requiring the ripping out of the toenail, was endemic. It was caused by the fine spray from the loom that was mixed with grains of brass and other metals thrown off by the machinery.

One witness to the industrial misery was the Rev William Murphy O'Hanlon, in spite of his name a Congregationalist minister from Lancashire. In a series of letters to the *Northern Whig* which he later published in pamphlet form in 1853 as *Walks Among the Poor of Belfast and Suggestions for Their Improvement*, he described the living conditions in town centre slums as 'crowded with human beings in the lowest stage of social degradation'. He revealed that even skilled workers might earn as little as one shilling and sixpence a week while those employed in the higher departments of the linen trade could earn from four shillings to six shillings a week in 'good times'. There were no trades unions; the latest Combination Act, on the statute book from 1825, prevented 'unlawful combining'. Cathal O'Byrne records how 'five poor tailors of that day' combined together and asked their employer for a rise in wages and were promptly sent to jail.

By any normal socio-industrial standards Belfast was an unlikely place to blossom into a manufacturing city. Apart from flax it had no natural resources, no coal, no iron ore and since it was dependent upon imports of raw material its port facilities needed to be at least adequate, which they clearly were not in the early years of the century. There was no deep-water anchorage; at low tide the Ormeau Bridge was unnecessary. Passenger ships from Glasgow or Liverpool that missed high water were stranded on the mud banks downstream of where the Queen's Bridge is now and travellers depended on freelance rowing boat pliers who would row them up to the dock 'in no time' for a shilling. After journeys of 22 hours most were glad to pay the fee. When the money was collected and the boat full, the ferrymen offered room for 'a few more at sixpence'.

The development of a proper deep-water dock was given to one of the most prodigious of Irish engineers, William Dargan (1799–1867). He was born in Carlow and trained as a surveyor with Thomas Telford (1757–1834), the great canal engineer and bridge builder. In 1831 he built the first Irish railway, from Dublin to Dun Laoghaire (or Kingstown, as it was then), and later laid the tracks for the railway to Carrickfergus on one side of the lough and Bangor on the other.

Dargan's excavation began in April 1839, authorised by the old Ballast Board that would have its name changed by the Belfast Harbour Act (1847) to the Belfast Harbour Commissioners. The old board had been as assiduous in its furthering of the port facilities as the Donegalls had been dilatory. The work was completed in less than two years, in April 1841, and the spoil from the cut formed an island known for eight years as Dargan's Island in honour of the surveyor. The new cut, known as the Victoria channel, was officially opened on 10 July 1849 by the chairman of the Belfast Harbour

Commission, William Pirrie. His grandson, also William Pirrie, was to play the most outstanding part in the history of this man-made feature.

The artificial island when it dried out became a badly needed park for Belfast people, with access by ferry at a cost of one penny for the return ticket. There the visitors could enjoy the glasshouses that were later transferred to the hitherto private Botanic Gardens. There were bathing boxes, gardens and a battery of mounted cannon for firing salutes on appropriate events such as the occasional balloon ascents that alarmed and excited the nineteenth century pleasure seekers. When Queen Victoria came to the town in 1849 the amenity was renamed Queen's Island and the site was to house Belfast's other claim to industrial greatness. With easy access to deep water and no likelihood of grounding on sandbanks because of 'the cuts', Belfast could now blossom as a port as well as a centre for engineering and shipbuilding, and its name in Irish, *Béal Feirste* ('the approach to the sandbank ford'), was no longer applicable. The debt to Dargan's ingenuity and skill was admitted again when, in 1994, a new bridge across the Lagan was named in his honour.

There had been shipbuilding in a small way on the lough from early in the eighteenth century. The first significant enterprise was that of William Ritchie, who started with wooden ships, but by 1820 had created the first Irish steamer. The hulk was still of wood but its power source was an engine made at the Lagan foundry of Coates and Young. Eighteen years later the first Irish iron ship was built for use in towing on Lough Neagh, not by a shipbuilding company but by the same engineering works. A similar move from foundry work to dock was that of the iron master Robert Hickson. His Eliza Street ironworks found it hard to compete with English and Scottish foundries that had no need to import iron expensively by sea. The Harbour Commissioners had by the middle of the century established the port with modern docks and loading facilities, and had a suitable site on the Queen's Island complete with launching slip. Hickson began to build ironclads there in 1853 aided by a new young manager, Edward Harland (1831–95).

Harland was from Scarborough and had got experience in engineering and shipbuilding at Newcastle upon Tyne, Liverpool and the Clyde. He worked hard and made the men work equally hard, going to the unheard of extent of banning smoking. He took over the firm in 1858 for £5,000, by which time the yard had completed four iron sailing ships, two steamships and a paddle steamer. Harland had obtained the large sum required to purchase the firm with the help of GC Schwabe of Liverpool, whose nephew Gustav Wolff (1834–1913) had been his assistant in the Island and was now partner. Schwabe was a partner in the Liverpool firm of Bibby & Co, the yard where Harland had worked, and was able to persuade them to place orders with Harland & Wolff of Belfast, as the firm was known from 1861. The yard was busy during the 1860s and in 1871 built one of the first White Star liners, *Oceanic I*, to an entirely revolutionary design. The relationship between the shipping company and Harland & Wolff was steady and to their mutual financial advantage. In the working partnership Harland was the shipbuilder and Wolff the innovative engineer but even more importantly the boardroom man with sound financial contacts.

Wolff's joking remark in reply to a toast:

> Sir Edward Harland builds the ships for our firm; Mr Pirrie makes the speeches and, as for me, I smoke cigars for the firm.

had a deal of truth in it. He had an easy expansive manner, his geniality in sharp contrast to Harland's terseness. In 1874 the firm took on a new partner, William James Pirrie (1847–1924), who certainly did more than make speeches. Under his eventual chairmanship, at the age of 27, the firm entered its golden age. The development of a new triple expansion engine in 1884 increased the speed of the ever more luxurious White Star liners making them the 'greyhounds of the ocean', the *Teutonic* built in 1889 crossing the Atlantic in a record six days, 17 hours and 25 minutes.

Wolff and Pirrie were temperamentally at odds, the latter eventually notorious for his dictatorial manner. Wolff had become a partner in the Belfast Ropeworks Company in 1873 and had transferred his business acumen, if not his total loyalty, to his new interest. He always could find money for the loans that the old firm continually required for development. Seventeen years later, at the turn of the century, the company was the largest in the world. Like Harland, who had a second career in politics, becoming Mayor of Belfast in 1885 and MP for North Belfast two years later, Wolff too decided to play his part in public service, becoming MP for East Belfast in 1892 and holding the seat until 1910. During his parliamentary career he was known as 'Teutonic', a tribute to his nationality since he was born in Hamburg, and to the name of the latest Belfast 'greyhound'. He returned briefly to the board while Pirrie served as Lord Mayor of the eight-year-old city in 1896. In 1911, two years before his death, he was made a freeman of the city and, musing upon his career, said, 'I had no idea when I came to Belfast in 1858 I would become a permanent citizen. I have no regrets I stayed.' He went on to quote a self-composed verse with an almost inevitable rhyme:

> You may talk of your Edinburgh and the beauties of Perth
> And all the large cities famed on the earth
> But give me my house, though it be in a garret
> In the pleasant surroundings of Ballymacarrett.

His house in Strandtown called 'The Den' was not exactly a garret in Ballymacarrett.

Though the firm never used his name Pirrie was the *real* Belfast shipbuilder. Born in Canada of a County Down family, he was taken home to Ireland by his mother, Eliza Swan Montgomery, on his father's death. An old boy of Inst, which he attended from 1858, he became the first 'gentleman apprentice' in the Island firm.[1] Pirrie was chief draughtsman when he became a junior partner in 1874, gradually assuming full executive power as the nominal owners took less part in the running of the firm. He married his cousin Margaret Montgomery Carlisle in 1879 and she remained fiercely loyal to his name even after his death. In 1899 Pirrie's yard launched four ships for the White Star Line, including the *Oceanic II*, at 17,274 tons the largest ship in the world. Apart from this prodigious output – he was the world's leading shipbuilder – he was an astute businessman, forming a syndicate with J[ohn] Pierpoint Morgan (1837–1913), one of America's richest financiers and railway owner, called the International Mercantile Marine. He opened yards at Govan, Liverpool, Southhampton and London and collaborated with the Danish firm of Burmeister and Wain in the production of marine diesel engines.

The apogee of his career came with the launch of the 45,000-ton *Olympic* in 1910, the world's largest ship, and a year later, the *Titanic*, a thousand tons heavier still at 46,382. These two vessels were floating palaces for first-class passengers but, as the inquiry after the disaster involving the latter discovered, not so luxurious for the third-class. The iceberg that ripped a 300-feet gash in the *Titanic's* hull on 14 April 1912, causing her to sink two and a half hours later, at 2.20am on the 15th, did more than cause two thirds of her passengers and crew to drown (including the same fraction of third-class children, while all first- and second-class children survived). The loss of the splendid ship on its maiden voyage all but ruined the reputation of Pirrie's firm, a catastrophe from which it took many years to recover. There were many mistakes of procedure, caused by the belief that the *Titanic* was 'virtually unsinkable', a claim made not by Pirrie but by the understandably euphoric *Shipbuilder*, the leading trade magazine. There were only 20 lifeboats and no emergency drills, and the watertight cellular system, now standard, did not work. The inquiry also found that no proper concern had been shown for the third-class passengers when disaster struck. It was the White Star

Line and its on-board inadequacies that bore the brunt of the criticism but the builders of the flawed vessel were also held deeply to blame.

Pirrie was involved personally in bereavement: Thomas Andrews (1873–1912), his brilliant young colleague and managing director, who was mainly responsible for the *Titanic*'s design, sank with her. His own health deteriorated and he had to conceal from his chief accountant just how heavily the company was overdrawn. His reputation and that of the firm were saved by the Great War. Pirrie's firm was vital to the war effort, producing warships, merchant carriers and eventually aeroplanes for the Allies. He had the special post of overall controller-general of merchant shipbuilding and succeeded in raising productivity in 1918 by 50 percent. A short post-war boom was followed by a general slump felt most keenly in the Clyde, Tyneside, Liverpool as well as in Belfast. The trauma of union struggles and the raw sectarianism of the early years of the Northern Ireland state he bore with stoicism but he forsook his early liberal support for Home Rule. The man who had chaired a meeting in Celtic Park at which John Redmond (1856–1918) and Winston Churchill (1874–1963) called for devolution was happy enough to accept a seat in the new Northern Ireland senate. Recurring illness had caused a kind of personality change in Pirrie. His accustomed air of authority had degenerated into autocracy and an imperviousness to rarely offered criticism by his managers. His death on board the *Ebro* on 7 June 1924 while on a cruise to South America left his successor Lord Kylsant with a near-bankrupt firm and the enmity of Lady Pirrie – William had been made a viscount in 1921 – who, having been made president of the company for life, would hear no criticism of her dead husband.

Another name in the history of Belfast shipbuilding was the 'wee yard' of Workman Clark which was founded in 1889 by a Belfast businessman, Frank Workman (1856–1927), in partnership with George Clark (1861–1935), who had come from Glasgow to work at Harland & Wolff as an apprentice. The epithet 'wee' is a comparative one since at its peak the firm had the sixth largest output in the world. It was sited further along the Antrim shore of the lough and, until it went out of business in 1935, it had built 536 ships, the last a marker to the future, an oil tanker. The firm's best year was during the post-war boom in 1919 when the 'wee yard' was second only to the big yard, sometimes known as 'Harassed and Worried' because of the size of the plant, the costliness of the operation and the susceptibility to depression. After the war and the birth pangs of the new Northern Ireland state the 'wee yard' was to be the scene of serious sectarian violence.

The fruitful interconnectedness of Belfast's chief industries was demonstrated in several ways in the city's industrial golden age. Wolff's other company, the Belfast Ropeworks, produced material that the shipbuilders needed and were pleased to have so conveniently available in the same 'industrial estate', as it would now be called. Wolff had the same proximate position in rope as he had in ships, the main dynamic coming from WH Smiles, the managing director. The latter was the son of Samuel Smiles (1812–1904), the Scots author of the Victorian lay bible, *Self-Help* (1859). As well as the finest strongest hemp for nautical purposes the works produced binder twine for the new reaping machines, sash cords for windows, fishing lines and the rope of choice of Charles Blondin (1824–97), the famous French funambulist, for crossing Niagara Falls with a man on his back. The firm began with only 100 employees but in its heyday it had 3,000 working in the largest ropeworks in the world, which supplied half the Royal Navy's cordage during the Great War.

The connection between engineering and shipbuilding is even more obvious. In a sense, under Robert Hickson, the iron founder, the shipbuilding industry grew out of ironworks. Between 1865 and 1900 the number of engineering workers increased from 900 by a factor of ten. The McAdam Brothers, off-site Gaelic enthusiasts, made steam pumps for irrigation on the River Nile. Samuel Davidson (1846–1921), a tea planter, took early retirement after inventing a process for drying tea in 1877. On his return home to Belfast he patented the invention and began, in 1881, the famous Sirocco works, called after the dry African wind but, because of Davidson's success, the word is now used generically as a type of drier. His fans were exported worldwide in those palmy days before the idea of a world war was conceivable, supplying the German navy with essential ventilation equipment in the build-up of the Kaiser's expansionist ambitions.

Another large foundry was that of Mackie's on the Springfield Road in west Belfast. The founder was a Scot, James Mackie, who had come to Ireland to install engines in a Drogheda spinning mill and had accepted the offer of a post of manager in the Albert Street foundry of James Scrimgeour in Belfast. In those years talent and courage were more obviously rewarded. Soon he owned the firm and when he died in 1887, his sons James Junior and Thomas took over the Clonard foundry. Their chief product was machinery for the linen and shipbuilding industries, design modifications achieved with great rapidity because of the ease of communication between manufacturer and neighbouring clients. Mackie's produced armour-piercing shells and machine tools for the forces in the Second World War and survived as a major employer until the end of the twentieth century.

Belfast remained a mainly Protestant town and during the mid-nineteenth century rather a Puritanical one, as we have seen, in its attitude to public amusement, especially theatre. This may have been the reason for a number of flourishing soft-drinks manufacturers. In a sense, just as Dublin was defined in the drinks world by Guinness, Belfast led the world in non-alcoholic beverages. A source of artesian springs was discovered early in the century at Cromac and, in 1852, Dr Thomas Cantrell began a soft drinks firm, joined by Henry Cochrane in 1867. The firm still flourishes as C&C.

WA Ross began his table-water company in 1876 and claimed to have invented the universal gin and tonic as a means of marketing his quinine drink. This was sold as a specific against the deadly tropical disease of malaria. Ross's tonic water was popular throughout the British Empire when a lot of the map was red. It was not alone; one Derry firm went so far as to label their product 'Antilaria'. Other successful firms were Grattan's, Corry's and the older Thwaite's. Ross's produced 36,000 bottles of soft drinks a day in 1889.

The hard stuff, however, was not neglected, especially in the years before Scotch became fashionable. By 1900, firms such as Dunville's, owned partly by the father of James Craig (1871–1940), the first prime minister of Northern Ireland, could produce two and a half million gallons a year from their giant distillery on Grosvenor Road. This complex gave the name to Distillery, once one of Belfast's best known professional soccer teams, in the game that had its Irish beginning in the city. As well as the Dunville output, the Irish Distillery in Connswater's two million gallons and the Avoniel Distillery's 850,000 meant that Belfast was responsible for 60 percent of all Irish exports of whiskey.

The other acceptable addiction was catered for as well, especially by Thomas Gallaher (1840–1927), who, born in Templemoyle, near Derry, opened his first tobacco factory in Sackville Street in that city and moved to Belfast in 1863, building the huge York Street five-storey plant in 1881 and enlarging it in 1896. Cigarette manufacture came late but from 1902 Gallaher's 'Blue' and the milder Gallaher's 'Green' continued to be serious rivals to Player and Wills. Gallaher was an energetic magnate, travelling the world to sample other tobaccos and finally purchased his own plantation in Virginia. He was almost the stereotypical Victorian master, paying his workers little and refusing them permission to join a union. He was chairman of the Belfast Steamship Company during the notorious dock strike of 1907 and by definition a sworn enemy of Jim Larkin (1876–1947), the workers' champion. Another tobacco firm was that of Murray Brothers, who identified the origin of their product by naming it Erinmore. To walk past their factory at the Boyne railway bridge, even in the late 1940s, was to experience passive smoking.

The plethora of successful operations and visible evidence of their existence made visitors to Belfast feel they were in a city rather like Manchester or Birmingham, with all the characteristics, good and bad, of nineteenth-century industrialism. The wail of factory sirens and the dense fogs that made the city so unhealthy were unexpected in an Irish town but the nearness of the country and the sea-lough mitigated somewhat the more pernicious effects. By the end of the first decade of the twentieth century it seemed that everything that Belfast industrialists touched turned to gold. The previous century had seen the intense little radical town turn into a megalopolis with all of the advantages of economic success for the few and a life not much above subsistence for the workers who made the desirable products. Class divisions became exaggerated in a way hardly noticed in the eighteenth century, with a burgeoning bourgeoisie enjoying the fruits of the trade boom, and a proletariat with too frequent deaths in children and low life expectancy in their parents. Slums, ill-health and the other attendant social evils marked the unacceptable undergrowth of the free capitalist jungle. These endemic evils that characterised the urban sisters – Manchester, Birmingham, Leeds, Middlesbrough, and to a lesser extent, London – had added to them in Belfast the further evil of sectarianism, which regularly degenerated into murderous violence.

6

Sectarian City

THERE WERE TWO CHARACTERISTICS OF LINENOPOLIS as the growth century progressed: poor working-class conditions and recurring virulent sectarianism. The first it shared with the other Victorian cities, the second was almost uniquely its own. True there were anti-Irish incidents in places like Cardiff and Glasgow and to a lesser extent Manchester and Liverpool. Outside of Ireland nationality rather than religion was the trigger. The Irish, especially those refugees of the Great Famine of the Hungry Forties, survived by taking the meanest of jobs and were accused of accepting lower wages than the natives. In Belfast atavistic fears and prejudice grew as the Catholic population of the city increased. The Protestant good wishes and financial support that had characterised the opening of the 'old chapel' of St Mary's in 1783 and that of the 'new chapel' of St Patrick's in Donegall Street in 1815 began to be dissipated as a significant number of the unpredictable Papists settled in the growing town.[1]

The census figures for the town for 1861 show that out of a total population of 121,602 there were 41,406 Catholics, at 34.1 percent, the largest proportion in the town's history until the beginning of the Peace Process and the prospect of the ending of the Troubles, by which time the proportion was 46 percent. The total population had had almost doubled from the 1834 figures of 61,000 with 32.3

percent Catholic. The chief causes of the increase were the natural growth in population because of a slight improvement to life expectancy, the growing industrial prosperity of the town and the inevitability of rural immigration. The total percentage increases over the next four decades were: 1871, 27 percent; 1881, 13 percent; 1891, 30 percent; and 1901, 36 percent. In those years the Catholic population remained proportionately rather static with a slight tendency towards diminishment: 1871, 31.9 percent; 1881, 28.8 percent; 1891, 26.3 percent; and 1901, 24.6 percent. By then the city had acquired an unenviable reputation for riot and sectarian strife. The English cities, to which a large number of Irish resorted, treated their influx as that of an alien ethnic group who were required to assimilate. Perhaps Catholics in Belfast formed the same kind of ethnic sub-group. Belfast was by comparison with other settlements in Ulster a young and essentially Protestant town in which, it was possible to argue, Catholics had no right of tenancy.

As noted above the radical tradition diminished and all but died. The people of the prosperous industrial town with ambitions to city status and the industrial muscle to achieve it were no longer anxious for independence. Any residual objection to the Act of Union vanished with the town's obvious economic superiority to other cities, even Dublin.

One of the great architects of Belfast acquiescence in being a part of the United Kingdom was the eloquent, tireless, and incidentally anti-Catholic Henry Cooke (1788–1868). The Presbyterian fundamentalist from County Derry could claim to have routed the liberal and radical wing of his church. His two great successes were the defeat in 1830 of the 'New Light' led by Henry Montgomery (1788–1865), driving with him the tatters of Presbyterian radicalism, accused unjustly of heresy, and the essential expulsion from the city of the Liberator, Daniel O'Connell, when he came in January 1841 to advocate the repeal of the Union. O'Connell refused Cooke's challenge to a public debate, wisely in the circumstances; his hotel and St Patrick's Church in Donegall Street were attacked by window-breaking mobs. He left Belfast escorted by many policemen, 'for his own protection'; they did not, however, protect Catholic protesters, who objected to bands of the newly revived Orangemen shouting, 'To Hell with the Pope!' Cooke's speech at a protest rally made two points – the economic advantage of the Union and the fear of Rome rule – unanswerable, at least to the ears of his supporters:

> Turn in what direction we will our eyes meet new streets and public buildings – numbers of new manufactories rise up on either side – and look where we may, we see signs of increasing prosperity… And to what cause is that prosperity owing? Is it not the free intercourse, which the Union enables us to enjoy with England and Scotland…? Can there be any religious liberty…where freedom of conscience is unknown?

O'Connell's lack of awareness of the true temper of northern opposition was to be repeated in other nationalist leaders from Parnell to de Valera. What MacNeice called 'the hard cold fire of the northerner' in his poem 'Belfast' (1931) somehow failed to make its way into their calculations. And any attempt at amelioration of the plight of Catholics was treated as inimical to Protestantism and met with violence.

One of the main sources of that violence was the Orange Order. It had been formed out of the faction known as the Peep-o'-Day Boys in opposition to Catholic Defenderism. The earlier conflict had been partially rooted in economics: Catholics had had the temerity to take part in the linen trade, known as an exclusively Protestant occupation, in the ultra loyalist territory of north Armagh. The other source of Protestant animosity was the series of relaxations of the popery laws. Succeeding chief secretaries, including Peel, tried to suppress the Order but it seemed to have the capacity for self-renewal, having a reincarnation in Brunswick clubs, called after the Duke of Brunswick, a Hanoverian kinsman of the queen. It came into Belfast as part of the rural drift townwards and, though originally Episcopalian in belief, asserting loyalty to George III and in deliberate contrast to the republican wing of Presbyterianism, it soon became a pan-Protestant organisation in deliberate contrast to Catholicism.

'Peace' between Presbyterian and Episcopalian had been achieved formally by Cooke when he published the 'banns of marriage' between the two churches at a great Protestant demonstration at Hillsborough in 1834, and in his anti-O'Connell rally in 1841, his audience had a slightly greater majority of Episcopalians. Whatever about the doctrinal aspects of the marriage the political union was secure.

A majority of members of the Orange Order remained working-class, just as in rural areas it consisted largely of peasants. It had some local aristocrats on its lists, a convenience when those guilty of riot and anti-Catholic affrays came to court since the accused were often tried and set free by magistrates who were themselves Orangemen. After the deaths of 30 Catholics in an affray at Dolly's Brae near Castlewellan in County Down on 12 July 1849 the reaffirmed Party Processions Act (1832) forbade the holding of provocative demonstrations and marches and Lord Roden, who was believed to have encouraged the affray, was censured and dismissed from the bench. The Order still persisted in different parts of Ulster and, after it found a champion in William 'Johnston of Ballykilbeg' (1829–1902), who continued to assert its right to parade, it resumed a confident existence. It received quasi-respectability when Lord Randolph Churchill (1849–95) in 1886 encouraged its virulently anti-Home Rule agitation and suggested that the Tories 'play the Orange card'.

Apologists for the Order emphasise the social aspects of membership and the pageantry and folksy elements of its events but in the North's largest town its appearance on the streets could often signal riot and anti-Catholic violence. As the century advanced the Order became the public face of Belfast Protestantism in its determination to keep Papists in an inferior position, economically and socially. An early manifestation in Belfast of its ability to generate, if not actually to cause, street violence was its attempt to march on

12 July 1813 through Hercules Street, a narrow lane mainly concerned with the meat trade and then a small Catholic enclave. It was almost an article of Orange faith that no path, road or thoroughfare should be closed to the marchers. Strictly speaking their demands were perfectly legal if not actually advisable but no one had the temerity to suggest that Protestant areas should be equally available to Catholics. Ironically, Hercules Street became Royal Avenue in the 1880s but in its heyday must then have been an olfactory nightmare. It was the dangerous exaltation that the anniversary of the inconclusive Battle of the Boyne (1 July 1690 – old style) often caused that made a triumphalist 'walk' through the small Papist district a necessary part of the day's celebration. It was ominous that in that year the something less than 4,000 Belfast Catholics, making up about 12 percent of the total population, should have become an irritant. A year later Protestants contributed to the building of the new chapel, St Patrick's, in Donegall Street.

The denizens of Hercules Street responded, as it was certain they would, with verbal violence and actual bodily harm. Two of the marchers let off muskets, killing two bystanders who were in fact Protestant. Four Orangemen were found guilty of unlawful killing and an equal number of Catholics were convicted of riot. The prosecutor advised the Order that they should not presume 'the title to exclusive loyalty' especially when they 'tend to disturb the public peace'. He was all the more discouraged in that Belfast had 'hitherto stood distinguished by the improved state of its civilisation and manners'.

Belfast was to be distinguished by other things: side-by-side with exponential industrial growth the town was to become notorious for intermittent, essentially ethnic, violence. One reads of economic and non-sectarian riots in August 1815 and January 1816 by weavers with something of relief. By 1832, with a population of about 56,000, a third of them Catholic, the ethnic mix was more volatile. Parliamentary elections were based on a wider franchise and when a victorious candidate was carried around in celebration, a Protestant mob attacked Hercules Street and four people were killed by the city police force, manned almost entirely by Orangemen. The following year, two mobs – one from the Catholic Pound Loney and the other from nearby Sandy Row – attacked each other at what later became the Grosvenor Road interface. This violence was repeated at the same flashpoint after the 1841 election and again in 1852 when with exquisite timing the election was held on 12 July. There was at least one fatality (not all such were reported), the military were called in to restore order and for the first time, in a pattern that was to be repeated, Catholics fled from their houses taking what possessions they could.

By the 1850s the town had received a steady influx of Famine refugees and had a Catholic population of nearly one third of the estimated total of 100,000. There were by now well-established 'Catholic' areas, notably the lower Falls, spreading from its heart in the Pound Loney, and finding work, usually unskilled, but not exclusively, in the Falls Road mills of such Catholic employers as William Ross. The 'Papist' area still included Hercules Street, Smithfield and Millfield, near where another Catholic employer, Bernard Hughes (1808–78), had his large bakery in Donegall Street. Hughes had been married to his Presbyterian fiancée by no less a person than Henry Cooke, with whom he remained on cordial terms and who was perfectly companionable outside of the stark May Street church that had been presented to him in 1829. Hughes's contribution to famine relief was eminently practical: he managed to produce a much cheaper loaf that blunted the great hunger. His name was still remembered in the twentieth century because of his famous bun that caused any person called Hughes to be nicknamed 'Bap' and for a not very complimentary rhyme popular with children:

> Barney Hughes's bread
> Sticks to your belly like lead;
> It's no wonder you fart like thunder –
> Barney Hughes's bread

Other Catholic areas already existed in nucleus: Ardoyne in the north-west of the town, the Markets area in the south, Short Strand in the east, where they were in a large majority, and Dock Ward, centred at York Street, where there was a significant minority of 29 percent. These Catholic parts lay close to larger Protestant areas in a kind of ghastly twinning that continued to seem menacing: the Falls with the Shankill, Ardoyne with Ligoneil, and Short Strand with Ballymacarrett.

In spite of political, cultural, religious and, in general, economic differences, the two communities lived in reasonable harmony for at least three quarters of each year. The celebration each July of William III's victory at the Boyne was often an occasion of riot but in quieter times Catholics enjoyed the ritual, the panoply and the music. Both sides of the house, to use the surprisingly domestic description of the separateness, were Christians and under biblical obligation to love their enemies. Yet even the most prosperous of Protestants looked back in fear of 1641 when the dispossessed had risen in bloody revolt. Catholics were not to be trusted; they were believed to be controlled and manipulated by a foreign ruler who could be the very Antichrist as foretold in the epistles of St John. Some clergymen, hating the sin and sinners equally, decided for their own purposes to whip up hatred of their fellow townsmen. Chief among these in the 1850s and later was Hugh Hanna (1824–92), who earned the literal epithet 'roaring'. His church in Berry Street was ominously close to a solid Catholic area and such was the charismatic power of his rhetoric that his Protestant listeners were easily inflamed and urged to action.

Even more inflammatory was Dr Thomas Drew (1800–70), the Anglican rector of Christ's Church, which lay literally at the heart of trouble and who was named as responsible for serious rioting in 1857. His address to Orangemen on 12 July of that year sparked violence that lasted for ten days. In his church, placed just on what would later be called a 'peace line', he had attacked 'the arrogant pretences of Popes and the outrageous dogmata of their blood-stained religion'.

Hanna's words on 6 September at an open-air meeting at Duncrue salt works caused further trouble. A commission held in November blamed Drew, the Orange Order and the Town Constabulary, known to be partial. It specifically criticised Orange events 'leading as they do to violence, outrage, religious animosities, hatred between classes, and, too often, bloodshed and the loss of life'. Its words were largely unheeded: Protestant Belfast, urged on by some of its clerics, was asserting its position as the Protestant capital of the Protestant part of Ireland.

Catholics were not on the whole extreme in politics; they were all too conscious of their political and economic vulnerability. They felt that if they behaved themselves and did not 'bulge' they could expect a low-level toleration. In this attitude they were joined by at least two nineteenth-century bishops of Down and Connor. William Crolly (1780–1849), who lived in Belfast from 1812 to 1835, when he was translated as archbishop to the primatial see of Armagh, found it expedient and even advantageous to support the system of national schools and even the proposed Queen's colleges. When he became bishop in 1825 he moved the centre of diocesan administration from Downpatrick to the town, conscious that the number of Belfast Catholics, at about 17,000, had become significant. He had many Protestant friends and served on multi-denominational committees. His immediate successor, Cornelius Denvir, who was bishop (1835–65) had partly, because of lack of resources and a sense of what the segregation required by the Vatican might lead to, also assented to at least a partial integration of education. He was berated for his caution by his fellow bishops but he was the man on the spot and perhaps wiser that they. This, as we have seen, changed during the bishopric of his successor Patrick Dorrian.

Religion and politics – if there was any difference in the eyes of the townspeople – continued to be the cause of recurring street violence. The 1857 trouble grew largely from the climate of heated evangelism but other causes soon emerged. Essentially the causes of tension and effectively racial hatred had been imported into the once liberal town by rural immigrants who dragged with them atavistic fears and resentments, most of them generated by folk memory with its tendency to exaggeration. Old stories of dispossession, penal legislation and resultant economic disadvantage, fear of another 'massacre' and the need for one side to feel superior to the other, all contributed to hatred. There was no alleviation of antagonism that normal intercourse in smaller towns at times managed – and often led to 'mixed' marriages. The two communities in Belfast suffered from endemic ignorance of each other's beliefs and social structures intensified by economic differences; Catholics were on the whole at most semi-skilled and usually unskilled. They were less well educated and promotion consequently eluded their children. Though the slums in Sandy Row and Peter's Hill were as bad as those in the Catholic Pound area, most Protestants looked to better themselves and, within the limits of *laissez-faire*, their Protestant bosses were happy to consider the possibility. The churchgoers among them, whether to the liturgically low Church of Ireland or the more austere Presbyterian meeting-houses, could be fairly sure of justification before the Lord, whose image owed more to the Old Testament Jehovah than to the church founded by Christ.

Their opposite numbers could identify with an all-Ireland culture, and with the inevitable if slow improvement in their economic position, happily espoused the growing nationalism, following Isaac Butt (1813–79) and the dauntingly successful Charles Stewart Parnell (1846–91). With such leaders the repeal of the Act of Union was no longer a millennial dream. The Liberal Party, under William Ewart Gladstone (1809–98), was going to try to pass a Home Rule bill that would restore a measure of self-determination to a country which because of a series of electoral reform measures had an overwhelming nationalist majority. The Belfast Protestant community, deeply suspicious of anything 'Romish', sincerely believed that 'Home Rule' meant 'Rome Rule'. They had not any clear idea of how influential the Romish clergy were with their flocks. Some even believed that the visible increase in the Catholic population – in 1861, the highest proportion for more than a hundred years in the future – was due to infiltration from the south. In fact the greater majority of Catholic immigrants came from the neighbouring counties of Antrim and Down, with very few even from west Ulster. As Belfast's reputation for riot and anti-Catholic discrimination became more manifest, immigration dropped so that the percentage Catholic population decreased from 34 percent in 1861 to a fairly steady 23 percent for most of the twentieth century.[2]

There were serious riots with widespread violence, involving death, injury and destruction of property in 1864, 1872 and 1886 and lesser outbreaks in 1893 and 1898. The causes varied. On 8 August 1864 a large crowd of Belfast Catholics marched through Dublin, led by Archbishop Paul Cullen, to mark the laying of the foundation stone of the striking monument to Daniel O'Connell by John Henry Foley (1818–74) that was to dominate Sackville, later O'Connell, Street ever since. As they left the GNR station in Great Victoria Street they could be thought to have constituted an illegal march, which enraged the Orange Order who at the time were uncharacteristically observing the Party Processions Act. A huge crowd of Orangemen constructed a libellous effigy of the Liberator and burnt it on the Boyne Bridge, the railway bridge that still links Durham Street and Sandy Row.

The Pound Loney that gave its name to the predominantly Catholic area in the riven town ran from there up past the top of Barrack Street to what was later Divis Street. The word 'loney' is a form of the Scots word 'loanen', a lane between fields. The Falls Road also has a rural connotation, coming from the Irish word *fál* meaning a hedge or fence. The town cattle pound and stray dog kennels were sited there, whence the name. The street was quite short but almost entirely Catholic and gave a convenient title to a much larger district that included the largest of Bernard Hughes's bakeries, the Model, and the stately and almost completed St Peter's

Pro-Cathedral. The Gothic-revival grandeur of the building, designed by the Rev Jeremiah McAuley, an architect turned priest, rising as tall as the surrounding Satanic mills was to more extreme Protestants further evidence of a rapidly increasing Papist threat.

Tension remained high. On Friday, 12 August Protestants stoned Bishop Dorrian's house in Howard Street and Catholics attacked May Street church, from where the outspokenly anti-Catholic Henry Cooke preached. On the fifteenth, the Feast of the Assumption, 400 Catholics navvies who had come to the town to build new docks gathered outside St Malachy's Church in Alfred Street, expecting a Protestant attack. When none materialised they rushed into the nearby town centre, looting material from shops, especially gun dealers. They surged on Peter's Hill and attacked Brown Street school, injuring some of the children. The mob returned to the Pound to recover. The closeness of the two ghettoes meant that no long journeys had to be made for confrontation. By 4pm the Sandy Row contingent had gathered at the Ulster Hall in Bedford Street, ready now to attack St Malachy's, less than 250 metres away. They were driven back from the church by gunfire from the windows but used the respite to stock up with arms and other hardware, obtained by plunder from town centre shops. Tuesday's target was St Peter's but they were driven from it as well by soldiers of the 64th Regiment of Foot. Frustrated again they crossed the Shankill into Malvern Street where they demolished the Catholic School there, as the principal said, 'calmly and deliberately… like furniture removers'. By Thursday, 18 August there were eleven people dead and many more seriously wounded.

The riots finally were quelled, not by the 1,000 members of the Irish Constabulary (the forerunners of the RIC), the several regiments of soldiers, including the mounted Hussars and some heavy artillery, and 150 of the Protestant Town Police – one of whom was arrested for throwing stones at the constabulary – but by heavy August rain. The trouble had persisted because for once the Catholics with the navvies on their side were rather more than a match for the

Protestants, even supported by many shipyard workers. The official inquiry heavily criticised the town's Conservative magistrates for making no attempt to curb the activities of the Protestant mob and insisted that the 'Bulkies', the nickname for the Town Police, the total membership of which contained only five Catholics, should be disbanded. When future disturbances should arise it was the Royal Irish Constabulary (RIC), 'royal' since 1867 because of their effective work against the Fenians, who had the main task of dealing with the riots. Extra numbers of this fairly impartial all-Ireland force had to be drafted in from the three other provinces, and sounding and looking (to those wise ones who could tell simply by sight) like Catholics, became obvious targets for the Protestant mobs.

The relentless animus against the Catholic quarter of the population had continually to be fuelled by those politicians for whom division and disunity meant power. In 1870 the formally anti-Catholic Orange Order, with over 4,000 members in more than 100 lodges in the town, had been given the freedom to march where they wished with the repeal of the Party Processions Act. This had been achieved mainly by the efforts of the Order's champion, 'Johnston of Ballykilbeg', and it provided an unfailing, at times quasi-paramilitary, support for Conservatism, throughout Ireland and in Britain.

The 1872 violence was sparked by a Protestant attack on Belfast's first Nationalist march to Catholic Hannahstown to call for the release of Fenian prisoners. It was held on Thursday, 15 August, afterwards regularly used as a day for Nationalist celebration, later usually involving the Ancient Order of Hibernians (AOH), an import from Irish America. It was led by the Presbyterian Joseph Gilles ('Joe') Biggar (1828–90), later to be Parnell's ablest lieutenant in their campaign of Parliamentary obstruction. He was physically unattractive and was referred to with witty aptness by TP O'Connor (1848–1929), Nationalist MP for the Scotland division of Liverpool, as the 'Belfast Quasimodo to the Irish Esmeralda', a reference to Victor Hugo's novel *Notre-Dame de Paris* (1831). The route originally included Carlisle Circus but at the request of the police it went straight to Divis Street. 'Roaring' Hanna had claimed that they intended to destroy his new church St Enoch's at the circus. A band of 500 shipyard workers marched on Carlisle Circus and attacked the police, now regarded as legitimate targets. That night they carried Hanna shoulder-high, perhaps now suffering from laryngitis, through the Shankill. A group from the Pound met their rivals outside the GNR terminus in Great Victoria Street, filling the casualty wards in the Royal Hospital, then in Frederick Street, off York Street. The attacking of churches, shooting of people on their way to work, looting of shops, practised with determination by both sides, set the usual pattern but the most ominous development that was to disgrace the town for years to come was the expulsion of Protestants from 'Catholic' areas and the much more thorough driving of Catholics from nominated 'Protestant' parts.

The growing organisation of Nationalism was another cause of fear and hatred among many Protestants. In the years of relative peace the majority of Protestant workers regarded Catholics as inferior because of their lack of skills and their undoubtedly inferior earnings. The Nationalist/Catholic population (the two denominations were virtually identical) had the advantage, morally and tactically, of being the underdogs with aspirations. They were aware that a majority of their countrymen were edging towards independence and they had hopes, as it proved vain, that they might share in that freedom. Politics, however low-level, were a welcome distraction, not to say relief, from their tough labour when work was available, their miserable living conditions and an unlikely betterment for their children. Though a beleaguered minority in Belfast they felt part of a real majority, even though they had probably a greater affinity with their brothers in Sandy Row than with the Catholic bourgeois of Dublin and Cork or the peasants of Kerry.

Protestants had the unacknowledged psychological problem of having to regard their adversaries as genuinely inferior and the fatigue of maintaining superiority. The correspondent of the *Daily Telegraph*, never a friend of Nationalist Ireland, when covering the 1872 riots, dismissed the people of both the Pound and Sandy Row as 'half-quieted savages'.

The Third Reform Bill of 1884 granted universal male suffrage and in the election of 1886 a Home Rule candidate, Thomas Sexton, gave Parnell 86 seats – the 86 of '86 – enabling him to hold the balance of power in Westminster. It was also the initiation into political life of Joseph Devlin (1871–1934), who by the end of the century had become the benevolent 'boss' of Catholic Belfast. Gladstone, the Liberal leader, had formed the honourable ambition of settling the long-running Irish Question and introduced the first Home Rule Bill on 6 April 1886. It was defeated when 93 Liberals led by Joseph Chamberlain (1836–1914) voted against the bill at its second reading. When warned of the viciousness of possible riots in Belfast, Parnell showed an incomplete grasp of the situation with his statement at a rally in Plymouth: '1,000 men of the Royal Irish Constabulary will be amply sufficient to cope with all the rowdies that the Orangemen can produce.' Perhaps if the government had been strong and united and the Conservatives, led by Churchill, been less irresponsible, 1,000 RIC men backed by 1,000 soldiers might have settled the matter then once for all. With Churchill's playing 'the Orange Card' and thundering, 'Ulster will fight and Ulster will be right', and his Belfast supporters, led by Colonel Edward Saunderson (1837–1920), hurrying not for the last time to purchase arms, there was bound to be trouble.

The trigger for this round of violence is traditionally taken to be the unwise remark of a Catholic navvy who, on 6 June, led a group who expelled a Protestant, saying that after Home Rule became law, 'None of the Orange sort would get leave to work or earn a loaf of bread in Belfast.' The yard men attacked, sending ten navvies to hospital and allowing the 18 year old James Curran to drown. In the violence that followed most of the confrontations were between

Protestants and the RIC. On 9 June a mob of 2,000 Protestants attacked the Bower's Hill barracks in the Shankill and in the indiscriminate gunfire that followed, seven people, including two women and a 13 year old boy, were killed. As Hanna described it from the pulpit of St Enoch's, they were 'seven martyrs... sacrificed to avenge the resistance of a loyal people to a perfidious and traitorous policy'. In all, 50 people were killed, 371 policemen injured, 190 Catholics expelled from the shipyards, 31 public houses (usually owned by Catholics) destroyed and £90,000 (millions in today's money) worth of damage caused to property. The violence persisted sporadically until September when the monsoon season dampened the rioters' ardour. The threat of Home Rule chilled more than Protestant workers. It was seen in the industrial city as disastrous for business; Pirrie let it be known that he would transfer Harland & Wolff to the Clyde should it became law.

The 1886 riots were probably the worst in Belfast in the nineteenth century but not the last. There was some limited Nationalist reaction in 1893 to the massive show of strength in the Ulster Unionist Convention held in the Botanic Gardens on 17 June 1892, when 300,000 supporters cheered at the words of Duke of Abercorn:

> You are fighting for home, for liberty, for everything that makes life dear to you... Men of the North, I say: We will not have Home Rule!

The following April, Gladstone's Second Home Rule Bill was passed by the Commons and there were celebratory bonfires on Carrick Hill, though everyone knew that it would be thrown out by the House of Lords. Gladstone resigned that year and, with the Conservatives in power from 1895 until the Liberal landslide of 1906, Belfast became quiet and industrially profitable again. The centenary of the rising of 1798 was celebrated in Catholic Belfast as in many other parts of the country. It caused considerable Unionist criticism but serious confrontation was avoided. By now Catholic Belfast existed as a kind of alternative inner community, dwarfed by a continually increasing Protestant population. It was seldom at variance with its clerical leaders, embodied in a series of energetic but greatly controlling bishops. Patrick Dorrian was followed by Patrick McAllister (1826–95), who became bishop in 1886. During his episcopate the churches of St Paul, Sacred Heart, St Brigid and Holy Family were built. By 1891 there were eleven Catholic churches served by 41 secular clergy. In 1857 the city had only five churches with a total of nine priests; yet the 1901 census revealed that there were 15 churches and 73 secular clergy.

The position of Catholics in Belfast was made somewhat awkward by the Tridentine insistence on church control of education, including that of the offspring of mixed marriages. It posed a dilemma in that separate education intensified the ethnic split in the population and aggravated the suspicion with which each of the adversarial groups viewed the other. For the 30 years when William Crolly and Cornelius Denvir were bishops, from 1835 until 1865, they did not have the resources to build confessional schools. They were temperamentally acquiescent in the non-denominational national school system at primary level, in operation from 1831, accepting a general curriculum with specific periods set aside for religious instruction which they did control, mainly by the appointment of Catholic teachers. After the Powis Commission (1870) they were given officially the control over curriculum and textbooks that they had been exercising for years. The diocesan seminary, St Malachy's College, and the secondary schools run by the Irish Christian Brothers provided male secondary education for those Catholics who could afford it. (In this matter the brothers were not exacting debt collectors.) Secondary education for Catholic girls was provided after 1870 by the Dominican sisters.

Both Crolly and especially Denvir were criticised by their fellow bishops for their slowness in imposing the Tridentine ideal and when, in 1865, Patrick Dorrian became bishop he applied the full Cullenite enthusiasm to Church control. Economic amelioration allowed him to establish the Catholic structures described earlier. It was typical of his paternalistic style that while still only coadjutor bishop in 1864 he should have taken over the five-year-old Catholic Institute and effectively dissolved it. It had been set up by leading Catholic magnates such as Bernard Hughes, John Hamill, John McKenna, who owned a large grocery business, the Read Brothers, who owned the Belfast *Morning News*, and Matthew Bowen, the proprietor of the Royal Hotel in Donegall Place. When its committee realised that Dorrian demanded the final say in all aspects of its running it went into voluntary liquidation in 1866. His view, and that of a majority of his fellow prelates, was that the social activities of Catholics were as much the concern of their clergy as their spiritual life. Dorrian's episcopal concern did not extend to national politics. In this he instinctively followed Vatican feeling that the clergy should not involve themselves with constitutional matters, though he did not seem to mind municipal protest about the economic welfare of their flocks.

Patrick McAllister, Dorrian's successor, took no particular political stance except publicly to disapprove of the disgraced Parnell and to do his utmost to support the *Irish News*, which was founded as an anti-Parnell daily paper in 1891. In time it was able to incorporate the *Morning News* that had supported the 'uncrowned king'. McAllister died in 1895 and his successor, Henry Henry (1846–1908), took a much more vigorous and public part in Belfast politics. He was concerned less with national matters like the recurring agitation for Home Rule than with local 'Catholic' politics. His establishment of the Central Catholic Club, known as the 'Three Cs', with rooms in Royal Avenue, catered for the better-off Catholics, who by now formed part of a measurable middle-class. It provided a convenient agency where bishop, priests and laity could meet and discuss matters of mutual interest. Henry was a gifted and deeply spiritual man but his personality was unsuited to popular politics. He was somewhat arrogant and impatient of inferiors, faults not unknown in the Irish episcopate. The Catholic Association that he founded in 1896 was to confine its political activity to purely local matters. In the redrawing of boundaries in 1896 the Falls and Smithfield wards had a clear majority of Catholics and the bishop intended to use his association to determine the personnel and tactics of the new Catholic representatives.

By this means he was able to control local politics until 1905. Like Denvir 40 years earlier he seemed to trust the Protestants to do right by Catholics in spite of *prima facie* evidence to the contrary. Under his control his middle-class councillors worked hard to ameliorate the conditions of their working-class co-religionists but complaints were regularly made that none of them lived in the Falls or Smithfield but comfortably in mixed suburbs where their religion and politics were not identifiable.

Henry found he had a rival, a consummate politician and a true son of the old Pound, born in Hamill Street in 1871. This was Joseph Devlin – 'Wee Joe' to friends and foes alike – and his life was dedicated to working-class Belfast in a way impossible for members of the Catholic Association. His story is the most significant of the turn-of-the-century city. It was during the riots of 1872 when he was one year old that the absolute ethnic cleansing of aliens from Sandy Row and the Pound Loney began.

Sandy Row and the Pound Loney are now matters of history. Described in 1780 as a 'long string of falling cabins and tattered houses', Sandy Row survived into the twenty-first century as a lively street of popular shops, many of its clients not sharing the politics of the area. It even had a cinema called, unexceptionally, the Sandro. It took its name from sandbanks at the north end of its S-shape and like the Pound Loney became the label for an area with many streets all sharing the same politics. Now many of the old streets have been redeveloped and the bright thoroughfare bears none of the scars of old hostilities. The Loney is long gone and regretted by many. One old inhabitant, Fr Desmond Crilly, a missionary priest, wrote a poem with many verses, recalling all the lost streets, called 'The Litany of the Streets':

BELFAST

Knocking down Pound Street made the senses reel,
And this will happen also to Plevna and Peel,
While Panton Street and Percy Street will fall with Quadrant,
And Ross and Raglan Street will be reduced to sand.

Bread and Butter

THE BELFAST OF THE TURN OF the twentieth century was the despair of Marxist theorists. The city seemed to have the ingredients of the perfect workers' revolution: a large underpaid proletariat, living in wretched conditions, a classic case of economic exploitation.

The explosion did not in fact happen for guessable reasons: a majority of fairly contented skilled workers and an ethnic sub-class regarding each other as the enemy and not their capitalist bosses. As ever economic improvement, however exponentially slow, provided a level of living above mere subsistence and with that alleviation the beginnings of agitation for better conditions. Protestant workers were marginally better off than Catholics. They had skills that the 'Taigs' had not and thanks to such institutions as the Orange Order were much better organised.[1]

Sectarian suspicion and strife should have been part of Marxist awareness since it was a classical method of destroying working-class solidarity. In the year 1891 the population of the city was 255,995, of whom 67,378 were Catholic. If we can take two-thirds of these as a reasonable estimate of working-class numbers then there should have been at least 170,000 people who formed an underprivileged proletariat. Their political inertia may partly be explained by lack of municipal franchise but for many years the Town Council was dominated by Conservatives. In 1842 the Liberals did not have a single seat, a situation undoubtedly helped by John Bates, who was a political agent of tireless ingenuity and unscrupulousness. His career as Town Clerk and Town Solicitor was marked by fraud but he survived until 1855 when, found guilty on many counts of malpractice, he resigned and died a few months later. He survived for as long as he did in spite of blatant corruption mainly because he kept his party in power. The domination of council politics by right-wing interests continued preventing any possibility of welfare provision.

Bishop Henry's Catholic Association, which dominated the two Catholic wards in West Belfast created by the 1887 Municipal Extension Act, were thoroughly conscious of their responsibilities towards their working-class fellow Catholics. Improvement in working-class conditions was necessary in both communities. By comparison with conditions in industrial cities in England, Belfast was slightly better off. Not all the houses were built 'back to back' with no yards and having to rely on communal lavatories, conditions that persisted until the 1960s in cities like Leeds and Nottingham as well as the giants of Manchester, Liverpool and Birmingham. Acts of the 1840s improved lighting and sewage and laid down minimum standards for all new housing, including the provision of a small yard and an ash-pit, the latter an obvious euphemism for a hazardous garbage dump.

One of the great campaigners for public health improvements was Dr Andrew Malcolm (1818–56), whose report in 1852 showed that out of 10,000 homes he surveyed, only 3,000 had piped water and a third lacked a yard. It was also clear to him that Belfast had the highest death rate in Ireland and probably in the United Kingdom. Apart from the endemic industrial diseases, mainly those experienced in the flax mills and ropeworks, the almost non-existent sewage system and its attendant diseases were responsible for low life expectancy, between 35 and 40 years for those who survived childhood. Life expectancy for the young, according to Malcolm, was nine years.

This was the condition of the town when the Rev WM O'Hanlon took his *Walks Among the Poor of Belfast* (1853), reported in a series of letters to the Liberal *Northern Whig* and afterwards published in book form. He confined his investigations to town centre areas where filth and overcrowding made life intolerable, particularly in the enclosed courts that had no privies:

> Let me first direct your eye to some of the purlieus of North Queen-street... plunging into the alleys and entries of this neighbourhood, what indescribable scenes of poverty, filth and wretchedness everywhere meets the eye... no pure breath of heaven ever enters here; it is tainted and loaded by the most noisome, reeking feculence, as it struggles to reach these loathsome hovels.

The prevalence of vice, as indicated by the number of brothels, seemed to cause these mid-Victorians more concern than infant mortality. One small entry alone had four notorious houses and half the surgical cases in the General Hospital (later the Royal) in Frederick Street were syphilitic. Protestants, because of greater skill and larger wages, had marginally better conditions though O'Hanlon's description of their areas was just as emetic.

By the time that Bishop Henry's Catholic Association had control of the Falls and Smithfield there had been some improvement in the plight of the very poor. The Catholic members had no voting power in the Corporation but with limited membership of some committees could achieve some improvement in cases of individual hardship. As ever in cases of inadequate, not to say partial or corrupt municipal administration, public neglect was compensated for by private benevolence. Such voluntary agencies as the Society for Promoting the Education of the Deaf, Dumb and Blind, and the Cripples Institute alleviated hardship a little though they were characterised by the cold charity that Charles Dickens savagely pilloried.

Church agencies tended to favour their own members and often required attendance at religious services as a condition of assistance. The fear that charity might be a guise for proselytism meant that Catholics were generally forbidden to seek help from other church societies and were expected to look to any welfare structures that their own religion could offer. These were usually provided by such religious orders as the Sisters of Charity and the Sisters of Mercy, and the lay volunteers of the Society of St Vincent de Paul, founded in Paris in 1833 by Frederic Ozanam (1813–53), a French academic who was beatified in Paris in 1991 by John Paul II. The society came to Belfast in 1850 with its first 'conference', the word used by Ozanam for local working groups, associated with St Mary's Church, Chapel Lane. Conferences were soon established in St Patrick's and St Malachy's, and in 1865 in the new Pro-Cathedral, St Peter's. The SVP, as it is now usually known, continues to be needed even today in spite of the Welfare State. Inevitably the ethnic separation of even relief agencies further intensified the barriers between the two communities but the SVP made and makes no distinction of creed for those who ask for its help.

'Wee Joe' Devlin, Bishop Henry's political rival and ultimate conqueror, knew the miseries of working-class Belfast from birth. He was born on 13 February 1871 in Hamill Street in the Catholic enclave of the Pound Loney. He was educated by the Irish Christian Brothers in their primary school in Divis Street, a few hundred yards away. This was his only formal education but at that school and in those years the standard reached was at least the equivalent of GCSE. He first worked as a potboy and then as manager of one of the oldest pubs in Belfast. Located in Bank Lane, off Royal Avenue, it was known then as Kelly's Store but now as Kelly's Cellars.

With all the relentlessness of the autodidact he drove himself to compensate for what he perceived as a lack of formal education. His friends were not safe from his demands that they would listen to his 'pieces of elocution', prepared for competitions at which he won at least one gold medal. He worked as a journalist for the *Irish News* and later as Belfast correspondent of the Dublin *Freeman's Journal*. Though a devout Catholic he deplored the ghettoisation of Belfast that grew intense during his boyhood and young manhood and which seemed to have been given church approval by Henry. He was a vigorous worker for the people of the Falls and Smithfield, as indeed were the middle-class members of the Catholic Association, but he tended to look beyond the Lagan to Ireland as a whole and concern himself with national politics.

John Redmond, the Nationalist leader, had worked successfully to heal the schism in the Irish Party after the fall of Parnell and was ready to achieve Home Rule when the time should come that the Liberals should need his support. He judiciously damned the Catholic Association as sectarian and recognised in Devlin a man of integrity and of greater political gifts than himself. He could not have asked for a better representative of 'our friends from the North' and did what he could to advance his career. However as a protégé of the austere and depressive John Dillon (1851–1927), Devlin required no further sponsorship.

He was returned unopposed as member for North Kilkenny in 1902 while canvassing in America and regained West Belfast for the Irish Party in 1906, the year when his Nationalists routed all the members of the Catholic Association in the municipal elections. This landslide was achieved by a political machine that has never been rivalled since. His ability as a debater and hustings performer was outstanding but it was dwarfed by his genius as a political boss. He had made a number of visits to the USA and while there studied the Democrat machine that had helped elevate the immigrant Irish. He virtually imported an Irish-American fraternity known as the Ancient Order of Hibernians that had been founded in 1836 to succour the Irish and to maintain links between the various Irish-American communities. Originally known as the Friendly Sons of Erin, it was usually non-violent but probably shared members with more radical groups like Clan na Gael, especially during the period of Fenian activity. Its members defended the original St Patrick's Cathedral in New York from attacks by the Know-Nothings, the leading anti-Catholic party, in 1850. Its membership in Europe was small but, after Devlin became national president in 1905, membership rose from 10,000 to 60,000 in four years and reached 170,000 by 1914 when it outnumbered its American fraternity by 70,000. Devlin held on to the West Belfast seat until 1922, having defeated Eamon de Valera (1882–1975) in the 1918 election when Sinn Féin secured 73 of Ireland's 105 seats. He was MP for Belfast Central in the new Northern Ireland parliament and at Westminster for Fermanagh and Tyrone.

The AOH, as it was universally known, was dismissed by the Irish Party as inert and clerically dominated. This was also the view of James Connolly (1868–1916) and James Larkin, then trade union organisers. It was essentially non-violent but in Belfast, at least, relations with the hierarchy were often strained. It gathered strength after Devlin's electoral success in 1905 but he had been at odds with the spiritual leader of Belfast Catholics and was often in danger of a metaphorical swipe of the crosier from Henry. Though membership countrywide tended to come from strong farmers in the country and at least lower middle-class in the towns, in Belfast its greatest strength was to be found among the working-class. It gave young men there an identity, social companionship, and the other legal and welfare advantages of its status as a friendly society. They had come to realise that because of the lack of opportunities for advancement even in the public sector, when all jobs were for the 'boys' (a convenient way of referring to Protestants, especially members of the Orange Order), they had to look elsewhere. They had literally nothing to lose by supporting Home Rule.

The panoply of membership with sashes and banners added colour to their lives and in this regalia the change from orange to its spectroscopic neighbour green caused the not unjust gibe: 'The Ancient Order of Catholic Orangemen.' Their public events, usually held on St Patrick's Day or 15 August, the feast of Our Lady's Assumption, did seem minuscule versions of the grander celebrations of the Battle of the Boyne on 12 July or – for the Apprentice Boys – the Relief of Derry on 12 August. Unlike the members of the older guilds, who were formally anti-Catholic, they tended to be middle of the road and essentially non-polemical. They had no particular animus against Protestants, preferring to use their energies to improve their own situations. Connolly and Larkin were right to suggest some clerical influence but any support was from individual priests who could see the benevolent aspects of the Order.

Devlin was careful not to seem anti-clerical and to accept any help offered by ecclesiastical agencies. Most of his followers were practising and sincere Catholics and were unlikely to brook criticism of the men and women who had done what they could to alleviate their plight. Shaken by the visitation of the Great Famine most Catholics accepted the strictures of Holy Mother Church in all aspects of their lives.

It was this devotion that social reformers like Larkin found slavish, especially since its acceptance glossed over manifest injustice condoned by the Church. The dock strike of 1907 was a significant event in several ways. Though ultimately a failure, like Larkin's resistance to the Dublin employers' lock-out of 1913, it succeeded in establishing the fact of membership of trade unions for unskilled workers as a norm in both cities.

The strike by dockers and carters in 1907 was the culmination of small disputes among the labourers in the linen, engineering, baking and printing industries. That year there were 3,100 dock labourers and 1,500 carters, a large majority of whom belonged to no union. 'Big Jim' Larkin was almost a cinematic character, tall, brilliantly eloquent, favouring a large Stetson hat. He was born of poor Irish parents in Liverpool and spent his early childhood in Newry with grandparents. He arrived in Belfast to organise the workers into the National Union of Dock Labourers in January 1907 and claimed to have enrolled all but 200 dockers and all the carters. Since it was Belfast his job was made more difficult by the fact that these occupations were riven by sectarianism. Protestants dominated the cross-channel docks where work was regular, while the deep-sea docks, where work was intermittent, was manned by Catholics. The employers' response to union agitation for better conditions and improved pay was to lock out the Irish hands and bring in workers from England and Scotland.

The move was organised by Thomas Gallaher, the tobacco king, chairman of the Belfast Steamship Company, who made Larkin his personal adversary. To Larkin, Gallaher was one snake that St Patrick had not banished. He called on all unorganised workers to support the strikers while Gallaher employed blackleg labour to move the goods that the 'free' dockers had landed. Pickets prevented movement of goods about the city and caused serious disruption to the city's trade. Even the RIC supported the dockers and revealed that they were not being paid for the many hours of overtime. Many of those who protested, mostly Catholics from the Falls, were transferred to other parts of the country and their places were taken by cavalry.

Larkin called a great meeting for Sunday, 10 August and had a publicity coup when 'Wee Joe' arrived to show solidarity with the workers, conscious that they included Orangemen. Next day mill-workers overturned two vans in Divis Street and stoned the soldiers and police. When on the Tuesday arrests were made in the Falls Road, fierce rioting ensued. The military fired on the crowd and two people were killed and many injured. When conciliators arrived from England, Larkin was excluded from the discussions, though he did persuade the carters to accept a wage rise. The dockers were not so lucky and gained nothing on their return to work but grudging acceptance of their union.

There was a brief moment when Catholic and Protestant overcame their age-old hostility to unite for their common good. Larkin optimistically thought that 'the old sectarian curse had been banished

r from Ulster'. It hadn't – but the sight of Catholic and
stant marching together was a rich and rare sight for the people
Belfast. During the strike Larkin had emphasised that workers'
solidarity should take precedence over sectarian loyalties. The essence
of his oratory was captured for literature by the Belfast writer Michael
McLaverty (1904–1992) in *Call My Brother Back* (1939):

> Supposin' ye got all the Orange sashes and all the Green sashes in this
> town and ye tied them round loaves of bread and flung them over Queen's
> bridge, what would happen?… The gulls – the gulls that fly in the air,
> what would they do? They'd go for the bread! But *you* – the other Gulls –
> would go for the sashes every time!

Larkin's coming to Belfast in January 1907 was not the only
evidence of a tiny fissure in the permafrost of Unionist rule in the
city. The YMCA Hall in Wellington Place was the venue for the first
ever Labour Party conference, held 23–25 January, with a social
evening on the Saturday, 26 January. Until the previous February the
group of the 29 Labour MPs in Westminster had been known as the
Labour Representative Committee (LRC); then they formally adopted
the suggestion of the leader Keir Hardie (1856–1915) that they be
known as the Labour Party. The decision to hold its conference in
Belfast the following year was approved by 177 votes against the 86
for Manchester. On the Thursday a large public meeting was held in
the Ulster Hall, at which Keir Hardie was the chief speaker. The
Labour Leader, not necessarily impartial, reporting the meeting on 8
February began:

> The great Ulster Hall which has often rung with cheers for Protestantism
> and the landlord ascendancy in Ireland never before resounded with such
> an ocean roar of enthusiasm as that which welcomed the Labour Party to
> Belfast on Thursday.

Hardie in his speech said with typical *hwyl* if less conviction that
he rejoiced in the meeting as a sign that the old order of religious
bigotry was passing away from Belfast and a new order of labour and

fraternity had begun. He ended with a quotation from the one poet who was acceptable to Ulster Unionists and Labour Party members alike. After all, Friday would be Burns Night:

> Oh let us pray that come what may
> At come it will come for a' that
> That man to man the world o'er
> Shall brothers be for a' that.

On the Friday evening there was an evening of musical entertainment hosted by the Belfast Trades and Labour Council in St Mary's Hall, the Catholic equivalent of the Ulster Hall, with music by the Belfast Branch of the Amalgamated Musicians Union, all perfectly kosher! One of the performers was Cathal O'Byrne, who would later become famous as an antiquarian expert on his adopted city. As the *Irish News* reporter noted: 'The hall was specially decorated and in a prominent place was displayed the inscription, "*Céad Míle Fáilte*".' The conference minutes recorded that 'the later part of the evening was devoted to dancing in which Mr Hardie and many other delegates joined'.

Devlin found himself at odds with individual members of the Irish Party, notably William O'Brien (1881–1968), the labour leader, and Tim Healy (1855–1931), the sharp-tongued anti-Parnellite politician who was the first Nationalist governor-general of Saorstát Éireann, during whose term of office the vice-regal lodge was known as 'Uncle Tim's cabin'. Their differences were matters of policy and not of personality. Healy christened Devlin the 'Duodecimo Demosthenes', a tribute both to his size and his rhetorical skills.[2]

Devlin's political career essentially disappeared with the success of Sinn Féin in the 1918 general election and the partition of Ireland, though he did retain his West Belfast seat until boundary changes removed the Nationalist majority. He was offered the leadership of the Irish Party on the death of Redmond but left the position to Dillon. Yet he probably had no real ambition to lead an old constitutional party.

Because he had publicly disowned the Easter Rising and successfully persuaded northern Nationalists to agree to a temporary partition after 1916, triumphant Sinn Féin wanted nothing to do with him and he was to play no part in the governance of Saorstát Éireann and was granted no support either from Cumann na nGaedheal or from its successor in government, Fianna Fáil. He tried to hide his anger at what he saw as the Free State's betrayal of northern Catholics. As he put it in the debate on partition at Westminster in November 1920:

> 340,000 Catholics… are to be left permanently and enduringly at the mercy of the Protestant Parliament in the North of Ireland.

But he was essentially a pragmatist and knew that he had no future in mainstream politics. His deepest love was for his own people in Belfast and he was tireless in doing what he could to serve them, alleviating their ills and bringing some cheer into their lives. In this, as in all aspects of his political life, he was essentially non-sectarian, helping working-class Protestants, who were among those who sent him a daily quota of 30 letters. His taking of his seat in the Northern Ireland parliament in 1925 was in tune with his innate constitutionalism but he suffered only frustration at a time when Unionist intransigence was at its greatest and confined his attendance at both parliaments to times when Catholic affairs were being discussed.

He died in Belfast on 18 January 1934, having spent the last 15 years of his life in the service of Catholic Belfast, especially those who lived in his home territory of the Lower Falls. His funeral was the largest ever seen in the city and, though he used his prodigious oratorical gifts continuously to excoriate them, Unionist government officials joined with those of all other Irish political parties to follow his coffin. He remained friends with his adversaries, happy to invite Sir James Craig to a night of greyhound racing in Celtic Park, in the heart of his green constituency.

He remains an enigma; though greatly admired by women, he never married. His treatment of them and their deprived children was parental, as he organised bumper seaside excursions for them. His most imaginative touch was an early example of what we now call respite care; he established a holiday home for working women in Bangor, giving a majority of them the only annual break they were likely to have. He was too a little bit of a dandy, shown in photographs and caricatures with a large orchid in his buttonhole.

8

'Damn Yeats!'

UNTIL THE RENEWED AGITATION ABOUT HOME Rule at
the end of the first decade of the twentieth century life in the city
was fairly peaceful, except for the flash flood of the dockers' and
carters' strike in 1907. More and more people had leisure to enjoy
the advantages and pleasures of city life, and some of the city's
prevalent Puritanism began to mellow; there seemed to be more to
life than six days of labour and an unco pious Sunday.

It is held by some that the years between the fall of Parnell and
the Liberal landslide of 1906 were a time of political vacuum that
was filled by intellectual and aesthetic energy. There may have been
some truth of this in Dublin and other parts of the south but in
Belfast it was rather an alternative kind of politics that stimulated a
kind of mini-literary renaissance. As in Dublin the new interest in
things artistic was confined to a small minority who had money and/
or leisure for such pursuits. Yet if Belfast had rediscovered at the
start of the new century some of its intellectual excitement and interest
in the arts it had unquestionably an implicit political stimulus.

For most people the pub, the music hall, the football stadium and
the excursion train were the popular leisure outlets and as the city
grew the number of amenities grew with it. As in other cities the
theatre grew more popular as its audiences grew more sophisticated

and the new wonder of the cinema had not yet begun to threaten the 'legit'. The 'flickers' or 'flicks', so called because of the unsteady lighting, were still regarded as a fairground attraction and not the art form that it could later become. A mark of the growing freedom of thought was a slight deterioration in church attendance – not enough to cause any of the pastors of the many churches represented in the city any real concern – and the beginnings of a respect for the entertainments that London, then the world's largest city, could send. Film shows became respectable when they were part of what would later be called ciné-variety, as an item in the music hall. Most of the films were made by the Lumière film company of Paris and first shown in Belfast at the Empire Palace of Varieties two years after its opening in 1894. Since films were silent there was no language barrier. Films also became a feature of Dan Lowrey's Alhambra, opened in 1872.

The earliest Irish films were made about this time showing street scenes from Dublin and Belfast, a fire-engine speeding to a blaze and shots taken from the Dublin–Belfast train. Ireland's first full-time cinema was opened in Belfast on 12 August 1908 in St George's Hall in High Street and by 1914 there were 15 'picture palaces', as they were called. The name was cleverly chosen since their promise was of an opulence and romance in notable contrast to the drab real world outside. The list of these picture palaces includes the Arcadian in Albert Street, the Queen's and the Electric in York Street, the Coliseum in Grosvenor Road, the Kinema in Great Victoria Street, the Shaftesbury Pictoria in Shaftesbury Square, the Picturedrome in Mount Pottinger Road, the Princess in Newtownards Road, the Shankill Picturedrome and the Lyric in High Street.

Companies like Vitagraph and Biograph turned out a whole range of 'flicks' from slapstick comedies to melodramas to Shakespeare. (At least with the last of these the captions came easy to hand.) Stars like the beautiful and talented Mabel Normand (1894–1930), Mack Sennett's partner and Chaplin's co-star, and Mary Pickford (1893–

1979), who specialised in adolescent parts, playing the twelve-year-old Pollyanna when she was 27, were as well-known to Belfast cinema audiences as their neighbours.

A contemporary photograph taken by Alex R Hogg (1870–1939) in 1912 (now part of a collection held by the Ulster Museum) shows one of these 'palaces'. The Kelvin occupied 17–18 College Square East, the name a tribute to William Thomson, Lord Kelvin, who had been born there in 1824. The film on offer was coincidentally *Rory O'More*, one of 15 films made in Ireland the previous year by the Canadian director Sidney Olcott (1873–1949). It was set during the 1798 rebellion and helped kill thereafter the stage-Irish stereotype in films, though the British authorities did not approve of its theme. Belfast filmgoers could see it at the first house at 7pm or the second at 9pm. There was also a matinée at 3pm. Programmes were changed on Tuesdays and Fridays and there were, of course, no performances on the Sabbath. Seats cost 6d (pre-decimal pence) or 3d, not all that cheap when you consider that even skilled workers earned only about £2 a week.

Cinema's golden decade was from 1916 until the coming of the 'talkies'. At first poor sound quality made talking pictures seem merely a fad and they had the disadvantage of language difficulty. Until the making of *The Jazz Singer* (1927) films from Russia, Italy and France were as welcome as those from Hollywood since captions could easily be written in the appropriate national language but after sound was seen to be the future, America began to dominate the screen. Sound films became hugely popular and since admission had become cheap relative to wages, they became the chief diversion for all but the very austere. And as such came in for the same clerical fulmination that used to be directed at the music hall and the theatre. The zenith of the cinema's popularity in Belfast came with the building at Finaghy of the Tivoli in 1953. Then there were at least 43 working cinemas in the city, often with queues outside for especially popular offerings.

The other great pastime, then mainly for men, was attendance at football matches. Professional soccer came to Belfast in 1878 when the manager of a Belfast clothiers, John M McAlery, came back from an Edinburgh honeymoon an enthusiast for the game of association football that was then well established in Scotland. He arranged for an exhibition match between Queen's Park and Caledonians, played at the Ulster cricket ground at Ballynafeigh at the top of the Ormeau Road. It was such a success that he was encouraged to set up the first Irish football club, Cliftonville. The Irish Football Association (IFA) was founded in the Queen's hotel two years later on 18 November 1880.

The game had existed in Ireland since 1866 when local teams were formed. Linfield FC, that became one of Belfast's premier teams, had originated among Sandy Row mill workers in 1866. Most worked for the Linfield Mill of the Ulster Spinning Company and they were allowed to use the company's dining-hall as dressing room and play in the company's grounds. It was identified with the Protestant inner city, just as its rival, Belfast Celtic, was with the Catholic Falls Road.

Celtic joined the IFA in 1891 and its green-striped jerseys became as identifiable as Linfield's 'Blues'. Its grounds, Celtic Park, off the Donegall Road, was known to its fans as Paradise and was in sight of Windsor Park, its rivals' grounds, off the Lisburn Road. As with Rangers and Celtic, the Glasgow teams of the same political hue, politics often crowded out sportsmanship. In the end the constant danger from visceral supporters of the other side proved too much for Belfast Celtic. The climax came at a match in Windsor Park on Boxing Day 1948 when Linfield supporters rushed on to the pitch and in the ensuing mèlée, Jimmie Jones, a member of the Celtic team, sustained a broken leg. The club withdrew from competitive football at the end of the 1948–9 season, leaving a significant gap in the sporting life of Ulster.

Celtic Park was also the site for Ireland's first formally laid greyhound-racing track, opened in 1927, but races were held in the city from 1907.

Other teams ready to join the IFA were Distillery (1880) and Glentoran (1882), known respectively as the 'Whites' and the 'Glens'. The 'Whites' took their name from Dunville's distillery between the Falls and the Grosvenor Roads and were supported by the owners of the plant, one of whom was the father of James Craig, the future prime minister of Northern Ireland. By the first decade of the new century there were enough first-division teams to make Saturday afternoon attendance a must for men of all ages and persuasions. By 1911 a city fixture could draw a crowd of 10,000 people and those who could afford it travelled by train to support their teams at matches in Newry, Portadown, Lurgan, Coleraine and Derry.

Belfast was the terminus for three main railways: the Northern Counties Committee (NCC) of the parent British London Midland & Scottish company, with its main station at York Road; the Ulster Railway that later was incorporated into the Great Northern Railway (GNR), with a terminus in Great Victoria Street; and the Belfast and County Down (BCDR), starting from Bridgend. The first track was laid from Glengall Street in 1837 to Lisburn, a distance of seven and a half miles. It was extended to Lurgan and Portadown in 1842. Lines to Holywood and Carrickfergus were opened in 1848, Coleraine and Dublin were linked to Belfast in 1855, and Derry was brought into the network in 1860.

Railways throughout the world were greeted with fulminations from the pulpit against the possibilities of immorality provided by trains, especially those with cheap fares on the Sabbath. In France it was: '*Chemin de fer – chemin d'enfer*' ('the iron road – the road to hell'); in Belfast, the clergy attacked the railway companies for 'sending souls to devil at sixpence apiece'. Clergy did not like the freedom and mobility that the rail network gave their charges, though in time they appreciated it for the amenity it offered, if only for Sunday School outings. By 1903 Belfast (and Dublin) could be reached from most towns by rail, and leisure pursuits increased.

For most of the period of the growth of the town's industries there was little need of civic transport. Owners and workers lived close to their factories, mills and yards, and the employees walked while their masters drove or were driven in carriages. On occasional holidays the townspeople took to Dargan's Island and later to the few public parks that were provided by the council. Botanic Gardens, in existence since the 1820s, was usually closed to the general public except on particular occasions but joined the number of public parks that were opened in the last quarter of the nineteenth century. The first of these was created in 1869 out of the Ormeau demesne, once the Belfast home of the Donegalls. Others followed: Alexandra Park (1885), off the Antrim Road; Woodvale (1888), between the upper Shankill and upper Springfield; Dunville Park (1891), at the T-junction of the Grosvenor Road and the Falls; and Victoria Park (1891), near the site of Dargan's Island, in the east of the city. The Falls Park (1879), the second to be opened, and certainly one of the most beautiful, came into existence because of an episcopal change of mind. In 1866, when land in the Falls Road was vested for an interdenominational burying ground, part of it was offered as ground to be consecrated for Catholic burial. Bishop Dorrian decided instead to purchase land for the purpose at Milltown on the other side of the Falls above the Bog Meadows, a wetland between the Falls and Lisburn Road. The rejected land became the park for west Belfast and the Bog Meadows is now called what it always was – a nature reserve. The great advantage for the Catholics of the Pound was that their funerals need no longer pass through Sandy Row and so avoided the insult and often the injury that they might meet on their way to the older cemetery of Friars Bush in Stranmillis.

These 'lungs' were necessary for the densely populated and packed city; indeed there weren't enough of them. The solid blocking of streets of redbrick houses had little to relieve the sense of a concrete jungle. Dunville Park, set among one of most concentrated areas of working-class dwellings, was tiny. Yet, as Sean O'Faoláin remarked about the city in his *An Irish Journey* (1940), '…you can get out of it quickly'. He realised this when he stood on Cave Hill and saw how beautifully set the 'approach to the sandbank' actually was. The land had belonged (of course) to the Chichesters but the townspeople regarded it as their unofficial pleasure ground, long before the formation of Dargan's Island. One commentator, Thomas McTear, writing about the beginning of the nineteenth century, noted that '…it was much more resorted to then than now, as it was quite open and free, and almost the only recreation ground of the people'. To be fair there were also the tiny Carr's Glen to the north, round the corner from Cave Hill, and the long Colin Glen to the west, stretching all the way up to Hannahstown. Until the mid-century, Cave Hill became the site, every Easter, of a kind of minuscule Donnybrook Fair until the clergy, sensing as ever that people were enjoying themselves, denounced it from altar and pulpit, condemning its racket, drinking and fornicating. Though the town grew more staid in the years after 1850, Cave Hill was still a favourite place for picnics, especially when tramlines were laid in the upper parts of the Antrim Road.

The first form of public transport were horse omnibuses, which took those who could afford the fare from the railway stations to homes built further and further out into the suburbs. The Corporation's bye-laws for public transport were published in 1868 and by 1870 there were regular services to such immediate suburbs as Malone and Fortwilliam. By then the advantages of a tramway system were becoming clear. In 1872 the Belfast Street Tramways Company set up a system of single-decker, one-horse trams which could move faster because of decreased friction. Six years later double-decker, two-horse trams gave a very efficient service as far south as the Ormeau Bridge and the Botanic Gardens and north to Dunmore Park. The fares, ranging from 2d to 4d, were, however, beyond the reach of workers. In 1885 the highest paid bricklayers earned less than 8d an hour and worked a 57-hour week. Mill workers earned a total of eleven shillings a week, while engineering and foundry workers got £1.10 shillings.

Early in the 1880s the English owners of the tramways company sent over Andrew Nance as manager and he was to dominate the city's transport system for the next 35 years. He introduced a five-minute service and a universal fare of 2d that quickly drove the horse-drawn buses out of business. The inner network soon linked up with the Cavehill and Whitewell Tramway (1882) that meant that holidaymakers could travel all the way to Hazelwood, as the urban park was called.

It was clear that the horse would soon have to give way to electrical current. The world's first powered tramway, running between Portrush and the Giant's Causeway on the north Antrim coast, went into service in 1883 but the Belfast Corporation characteristically dragged its feet. It refused Nance's offer of the Belfast Street Tramways Company for £63,000 and the result was that Belfast was the last of the major cities, with which it was so often compared, to establish electric traction. It was not until 5 December 1905 that Belfast's first electric trams appeared and, unremarkably, the head of the company was the unsinkable Andrew Nance. Suddenly the population was mobile. The company carried one million passengers in 1881; by 1891 the number had been multiplied by ten and in 1904, 28 million journeys were made, mostly in from and out to the ring of new villas and better terraces where the city's growing lower middle-classes had found homes.

One of Nance's most important extensions was the Queen's Road tramway that carried the 14,000 Islandmen to and from work. Eighty cars were needed, running from well before 8am and reaching a peak between 5 and 7pm. They joined the chorus of morning sounds of early twentieth-century Belfast (except, of course, on Sundays), as Louis MacNeice recalled in his poem 'Carrickfergus' (1937), '...the hooting of lost sirens and the clang of trams'. The Island trams were the last to run in the city, stopping finally on Saturday, 27 February 1954. The Belfast 'gondolas' were no more; no more would a ride in the front seat of the upper deck on a stormy winter night, as the car rattled and hissed and swayed down the Grosvenor Road, seem like a trip in a lifeboat in a force-eight gale. Not just ecologists but town planners even now regret that these charming 'green' conveyances were not preserved and modernised to ease city-centre traffic congestion.

Also ecologically preferable to the diesel buses that replaced them were the trolleybuses that were intended to make the trams obsolete. They were silent and stable, except when sometimes on corners they, like the trams, would lose power if the rods that connected them to the overhead cables should become detached. These also needed to be changed at the terminuses on to the return lines. The first trial of the silent giants was on the Falls Road route in 1938 and it proved so successful that the Corporation decided to replace all the tramways, expecting to finish the conversion by 1944 at a cost of £1.25 million. The war intervened but when peace broke out the process continued. The Antrim Road tram became the Glengormley trolleybus in the spring of 1949. For a while trams, buses and trolleys coexisted but because of the obvious flexibility of the bus the days of electric transport were numbered. The trolleys outlasted the trams by 14 years and the power lines that had formed a kind of horizontal spider's web over the city's main roads disappeared in 1968 just as the tramlines and square setts had vanished earlier.

One other means of transport has unique associations with Belfast. Bicycles of one form or another had been in existence since the Babylonian empire that was at its height, c. 1790 BC. The first modern chain-drive bicycle was invented in 1874 and mass-produced in 1885. Tires were of solid rubber and tended to jolt the rider, especially over Belfast's cobbled streets. John Boyd Dunlop (1840–1921), a veterinary surgeon living in Gloucester Street, off Victoria Street, was to change that.

He came from his home in Ayrshire to set up his practice in Belfast and he had an ailing son who was advised to cycle to strengthen his weak chest. His rubber-tired tricycle tended to bounce him about too much. His inventive father experimented and finally produced a workable pneumatic tyre that on its initial trial, on 28 February 1888, allowed the happy Johnny a smooth ride. Dunlop sold his patent and factories in 1896 for three million pounds. With that improvement the 'bike' became a highly efficient means of individual transport and many who found the cost of train fares oppressive could travel conveniently about the relentlessly growing city and pedal out to Helen's Bay and Bangor on the south side of the lough, and Whitehead and even Islandmagee on the north.

In the 'quiet' years before Home Rule reared its divisive head after 1910 the city could be a very pleasant place. The workers were still underpaid and unhealthy because of industrial ailments and the countrywide endemic tuberculosis (called then 'phthisis'). But if you were not of the overworked class and had reasonable health, life, especially in the Edwardian decade, was really rather pleasant. Food, transport, newspapers and magazines, cigarettes, tobacco and snuff were cheap and plentiful. Victorian primness was thawing and the New Woman, wearing bloomers when she cycled, was asserting her independence and beginning to be affected by the English suffragettes who were demanding votes for women.

Greater leisure meant more time for intellectual, aesthetic and even national interests. Theatre in mid-Victorian Belfast had been greatly suspect, and a mark of gradually increased sophistication was a return of 'respectable' people to the play. This had been caused partly by the news that Queen Victoria, not the merriest of monarchs, was a regular playgoer. Lower tastes were catered for at the Empire in Victoria Square, the Alhambra in North Street, and the Alexandra at the corner of the Grosvenor Road and Durham Street, which supplied vaudeville items and melodramas like the periennial *Maria Marten, or The Murder in the Red Barn* (1830), based upon an actual murder case in Suffolk, the dramatisation of Mrs Henry Wood's (1814–87) novel *East Lynne*, and the ever-popular Irish works of Dion Boucicault (1820–90), especially *The Colleen Bawn*

(1860), also based upon an actual killing, this time in County Limerick.

Though a more respectable theatre already existed – the Theatre Royal in Arthur Street – JF Warden (1836–98), the leading impresario of the day, and himself manager of the Royal, wanted a new one that would be free of any hint of doubtful reputation that must still cling to any older Belfast theatre. He had prepared his growing bourgeois audience for better things by bringing, for example, the great Henry Irving (1838–1905) in the extremely melodramatic *The Bells* (1871) in tandem with his unforgettable Shylock in *The Merchant of Venice*, and Barry Sullivan (1821–1891), the leading Irish tragedian of the day (though born in London), who claimed to have played Richard III 2,500 times. He also encouraged seasons from the Carl Rosa opera company, founded by a German impresario, Carl Rose (1842–89), and the newly formed company of Richard Doyle McCarthy (1844–1901) (or as he preferred to be known, D'Oyly Carte) that brought the funny but highly revered comic operas of WS Gilbert (1836–1911) and Arthur Sullivan (1842–1900). Gilbert's own ambition was to make theatre respectable again, and *Trial by Jury* (1875) and *HMS Pinafore* (1878) began an immensely popular sequence.

Warden had already built the Royal Opera House in Derry and on the nearest Sunday to the opening, in August 1877, a sermon was preached by the Rev Robert Craig in Great James's Street Presbyterian Church indicating some displeasure at the prospect:

> You know it is a fact that many in the audience are the very scum and offscourings of the community – thieves and drunkards, spendthrifts and profligates – designing men and lost women. How few are the pure and good in comparison with the unclean and reprobate who crowd the doorways and fill the pit and galleries.

It was this attitude that Warden had to deal with. His solution was the Grand Opera House and Cirque, a gorgeous structure designed by the famous Frank Matcham (1854–1920), who built nearly a score of Britain's most opulent theatres, set in Great Victoria

Street. It opened on 23 December 1895, with seating for 2,500 people and should have had a career as glorious as its fabric. The truth is that Belfast did not take it to its heart and it had rather mixed fortunes. It became the Palace of Varieties in 1904 but reverted to its original function as an all-purpose entertainment house featuring ballet, opera, drama and pantomime, with an occasional film. During the Second World War, because of travel restrictions, it was the home of a twice-nightly resident repertory company called the Savoy Players, whose star Guy Rolfe (1911–2003), once a boxer and racing-driver, became a leading British film actor.

At a later stage it was in danger of demolition until it was saved after a campaign by the Ulster Architectural Heritage Society and listed as a building of architectural merit. It was refurbished by its new owner, the Arts Council of Northern Ireland. Surviving two bomb attacks and now run by an independent charitable trust it remains one of Belfast glories. Its theatrical neighbour, the Royal Hippodrome (1907–97) had a similar career as theatre, cine-variety and cinema, becoming a car park in 1996. Now it is part of the Opera House complex and houses bars, restaurants and a studio space called, rather unfortunately, the Baby Grand.

Edwardian Belfast was then well supplied with a variety of places of entertainment. Dublin's several Theatre Royals, the Queen's, the Gaiety and Olympia and others offered the same kind of local and largely imported entertainments that attracted, on the whole, larger audiences used to a theatrical tradition at least two hundred years old. It was as an alternative to this commercial, largely English, touring theatre that William Butler Yeats (1865–1939) and Lady Augusta Gregory (1852–1932) and the other stalwarts of the Irish Literary Renaissance established the Irish Literary Theatre (ILT) that finally found a permanent home in the Abbey thanks to the bounty of the Quaker tea heiress Annie Horniman (1860–1937). Some denizens of intellectual and aesthetic Belfast felt that they too were entitled to share in the literary revival that had seemed to galvanise the artistic life of the capital. It fact, it was a minority interest made all the more limited in its general effect since its sponsors were mainly Protestant.

It was a Quaker nationalist, Bulmer Hobson (1883–1969), who led Belfast's drive for an alternative theatre. He was one of a number of Protestants who found the industrial star of the Empire insufficiently Irish. He was a member of the Gaelic League, a Gaelic Athletic Association (GAA) organiser, founder of the Dungannon Clubs with Denis McCullough (1883–1968) and an early supporter of Arthur Griffith (1871–1922). His politics inevitably clashed not only with those of the Unionist establishment but also with John Redmond's.

His interest in drama was part of his twin political and cultural thrust. In 1902, when he and his companion David Parkhill were barely 20, they decided to put on in Belfast two of the ILT's plays, Yeats's *Cathleen Ni Houlihan* (1902) and *The Racing Lug* (1902) by the Belfast author James H[enry Sproull] Cousins (1873–1956). The Yeats play, set in Killala during the 1798 rising, had the sort of dramatic theme that Hobson wished to present to encourage the faint flame of nationalism that was beginning to show itself in the sectarian city. It was believed by its author, rather vaingloriously, to have a potentially powerful effect. As he wrote in the poem 'Man and the Echo', 'Did that play of mine send out/Certain men the English shot?' The young men from the North found the Dublin people very cordial, with the notable exception of Yeats, who was 'haughty and aloof' and refused permission. Maud Gonne, as ever dismissive of 'Willie', assured them, 'He wrote that play for me and gave it to me. It is mine and you can put it on whenever you want to.' That permission came later and, as the train steamed out of Amiens Street station, Hobson hit the arm of his seat and said, 'Damn Yeats, we'll write our own plays!' And they did.

The Ulster Literary Theatre (ULT) – the title a nod to the Dublin origins; they called it first 'The Ulster Branch of the Irish Literary Theatre' – began its life with the Dublin player Dudley Digges (1879–

1947), who afterwards had a successful career in Hollywood, appearing in the chosen plays. The venue was St Mary's Minor Hall, off Royal Avenue, and successful as the ULT turned out to be they never found a permanent home, using mainly the Grand Opera House for the 51 original plays that the venture generated in its 30 years of existence.

Probably the best remembered plays are those by 'Rutherford Mayne', the stage name of Samuel J[ohn] Waddell (1878–1967), brother of the scholar Helen Waddell (1889–1965), namely *Turn of the Road* (1906) and *The Drone* (1908); the satirical work of 'Gerald MacNamara' (Harry C Morrow) (1866–1938) with two very effective squibs, *The Mist That Does Be On the Bog* (1909), a send-up of the Synge-song of the Abbey plays, and *Thompson in Tír na nÓg* (1912), in which an Orangeman finds himself in the Gaelic Valhalla, 'The Land of Youth'. Other playwrights that had their first work presented by the ULT were Leslie A[lexander] Montgomery (1873–1961), using the cod pseudonym Lynn C Doyle, from the wood preservative, but later reverting to the simple Lynn Doyle for his many comic books and novels about Ulster, and George Shiels (1886–1949) (as George Morshiel), who kept the Abbey solvent with 30 popular plays written between 1922 and 1948.

The ULT also produced four issues of a journal called *Ulad*, the Irish word for the province of Ulster, but with an aspiration mark above the 'd' to give the word its proper final sound of 'oo'. Edited by Hobson and the Belfast poet Joseph Campbell (Seosamh Mac Cathmaoil) (1879–1944), author of 'My Lagan Love', it was published between November 1904 and September 1905, and was intended to indicate the part that Ulster might play in the literary revival. It was modelled on *Beltaine* (1899–1900) and *Samhain* (1901–6), produced by Yeats and the other Abbey dramatists.

Each copy of *Ulad* contained the text of one of the ULT's plays and essays by such contributors as Roger Casement (1864–1916), who was executed for his part in the 1916 rising, his friend Robert

Lynd (1879–1949), who, though living in London, wrote most of the text of the *Republic* (1906–7), the Dungannon Clubs' journal, Alice Milligan (1866–1953), the poet and editor with Ethna Carbery (1866–1902) of the *Shan Van Vocht* (1896–9), the Belfast literary journal, and other leading Irish writers, including Stephen Gwynn (1864–1950), Æ (1867–1935), Padraic Colum (1881–1972) and the reclusive Belfast novelist, Forrest Reid (1875–1947) .

The discovery of vibrant if limited cultural activity in the city, that Dublin and London intellectuals and aesthetes tended to dismiss as a mere Irish Manchester, was cheering if not exactly earth-shaking. It made little impression, as did any such 'highbrow' stuff, on the population at large. As far as the rich were concerned this discovery of an 'Irish' culture, however safely 'Ulsterised', savoured too much of Nationalism. The association of the politically doubtful Hobson with this Ulster renaissance did it no favours in Establishment eyes, but they felt that there was little harm in the movement or in the activities of the Gaelic League. As long as the Edwardian city remained Linenopolis or even Nauopolis, since ships were as important as fabric to the city's economic security, there was no reason for alarm. It was consoling, too, that most of those involved were respectable Protestants who should be able to realise on which side their bread was buttered. While the conditions that had produced such success were not in question some little indulgence could be granted to the plays and poems, but should anything arise that might upset that satisfactory and profitable status quo then attitudes would have to change.

9

City of the Covenant

HOBSON'S VARIOUS VENTURES, INCLUDING THOSE ostensibly concerned with matters aesthetic and recreational, were in fact innately political. Though the Gaelic League, from its inception on 31 July 1893, continued to emphasise its non-sectarian, non-political character, its stated aim of restoring Irish as a living language was implicitly nationalist and implied a future break with Britain. The two founders, Douglas Hyde (1860–1949), later first president of Ireland, and Eóin MacNeill (1867–1945), were academics but though Hyde continued to emphasise the League's detachment from contemporary politics MacNeill prepared it as an agency of possible revolution. For the first 20 years of its existence Hyde succeeded in preserving the non-political ideal and recreated Irish as an alternative language but after MacNeill founded the Irish Volunteers in 1913 the League's evolved purpose became clear.

Hobson was aware of the League's revolutionary potential from its foundation. He had joined the Irish Republican Brotherhood (IRB), the residuum of Fenianism, with his friend Denis McCullough and by 1907 was vice-president of Arthur Griffith's Sinn Féin. As a member of MacNeill's Irish Volunteers he was one of the organisers of the Howth gun-running in May 1914, the Volunteers' response to the much larger landing of weapons for the Ulster Volunteer Force

(UVF) a month earlier. His revolutionary tactics consisted mainly of civil resistance – he remained at heart a disciple of Griffith – and he would have used the Volunteers only in a guerrilla defensive role. He did all he could, therefore, to prevent 'a small junta within the IRB' planning the full-scale rising that happened at Easter 1916. To this end he warned MacNeill of its imminence, who immediately countermanded the order. Hobson himself was kept a virtual prisoner until Easter Monday, 24 April. After this clash of wills he took no further part in politics but joined the civil service of the new Free State, serving in the Revenue Commission from 1922 until his retirement in 1948. His interest in theatre continued; he was pleased to serve on the board of the Gate Theatre in Dublin. His autobiography, *Ireland, Yesterday and Tomorrow* (1968), written the year before his death, is a witty account of a remarkable life.

The dedication of Ulster Protestants like McCullough and Hobson to Irish nationalism showed that beneath the relative peace of the city a new interest in the repeal of the Act of Union was growing. It was partly stimulated by the centenary celebration of the rising of 1798 when the radical town's involvement with the Society of United Irishmen was recalled, and by the sense of a coming agitation again about Home Rule.

After its foundation in 1884 some Belfast Protestants began to take an interest even in the GAA games; hurling because of its skill and speed, and football perhaps because of its links with rugby. The more strictly sabbatarian among them deplored Sunday games and others objected to the equally Puritanical ban on playing, or even watching, 'foreign' games. The GAA's scarcely concealed links with Fenianism pleased some Catholics and greatly displeased others, including the hierarchy, and it did not then displace the affection and vigorous support that the city had always shown for soccer.

A number of Protestant scholars and antiquarians, inheritors of the traditions of McAdam, welcomed the Gaelic League and applauded the remarkable energy and organisation of its members.

One of these was Francis Joseph Bigger (1863–1926), who trained as a solicitor but dedicated his life to Irish archaeology and the Irish language. It was he who commissioned the monolith placed on the supposed grave of the premier Irish saints in the grounds of Downpatrick Cathedral. As the old rhyme has it: 'In Down three saints one grave do fill/Brigid, Patrick and Colum Cille.' His restoration of old castles and churches would nowadays be regarded as naïve but he felt he was making a serious contribution to a vanishing Irish heritage. The refurbished Ardglass Castle became a centre for Irish gatherings. As the historian Alice Stopford Green (1848–1924) put it in her book, *The Old Irish World* (1912):

> The castle was left absolutely to the people. Anyone who would came in. They sang, and sang, the sorrowful decadent songs of modern Ireland – songs of famine, emigration, lamentation, and woe. But still they sang of Ireland.

He had the remains of Henry Joy McCracken re-interred in the grave of his sister Mary Ann in Clifton Street graveyard. His house on the Antrim Road he made into a meeting place for like-minded enthusiasts and his library of more than 3,000 volumes became the nucleus of the Belfast Central Library's Irish collection. His interest in Irish music and song drove him to collaborate with Roger Casement in running *Feis na nGleann* in County Antrim in 1904 and he edited the *Ulster Journal of Archaeology* from 1894 until his death. Perhaps the greatest, if rather oblique, tribute to him was that his grave in Mallusk, his birthplace, was blown up by loyalists in the late 1970s.

The surge in interest in Irish history, language and heritage in Belfast was part of a countrywide phenomenon, as much a product of the relative peacefulness of the first decade of the new century as of a political vacuum. The first signs of change came with the Liberal landslide in the general election of 1906. It brought little change in Belfast except that 'Wee Joe' managed to win West Belfast by a majority of 16 votes. The new government had inherited a commitment from Gladstone's time to grant some form of Home

Rule to Ireland but they were so anxious to proceed with their social legislation that they kept postponing legislation even after H[erbert] H[enry] Asquith (1852–1928) became prime minister in 1908. They believed, and so did the electors, that the Old Age Pensions Act (1908) and the National Insurance Act (1910) took precedence over any attempt at settlement of the old and wearisome Irish Question. However, after the two elections of 1910, in January and December, the Liberals held power only by virtue of the cooperation of the Irish Party and, once David Lloyd George (1863–1945) succeeded with his Parliament Act (1911) in curtailing the power of the Lords and removing from them the power of veto of acts passed by the Commons, Home Rule was again rearing its troublesome head.

Even the slightest whiff of devolvement of powers was enough to set the hypersensitive Unionist antennae twitching. In 1904 the foundation by the southern Unionist, Lord Dunraven (1841–1926), of the Irish Reform Association that called for limited devolution produced almost immediately the resignation of the Chief Secretary George Wyndham and the formation of the Ulster Unionist Council that held its first formal meeting in March 1905. Its 200 members had 50 representatives from the Orange Order and 50 Ulster members of parliament. Its temporary unpaid secretary was a Belfast solicitor called [Richard] Dawson Bates (1876–1949), possibly the most extreme of all Unionists, whose temporary appointment lasted for 15 years and who later had a career as Northern Ireland's sternest Minister of Home Affairs.

Not entirely coincidentally 1905 also saw the foundation of the Dungannon Clubs that evolved into the northern Sinn Féin. Hobson chose the title as a tribute to the eighteenth-century Irish Volunteers and their two conventions held in that town in 1782 and 1783 to fight for parliamentary reform.

Until the formation of the council there had been dissension in Unionist ranks, evidenced by the setting up in 1902 of an Independent Orange Institution by Tom Sloan, a shipyard worker and fiery orator. Yet once the threat of Home Rule/Rome Rule was sensed Belfast Protestants forgot their differences and united to defend 'the old cause/That gave us our freedom, religion and laws', to quote the not entirely comic song, 'The Ould Orange Flute'.

The fear of Rome rule increased with the promulgation in 1908 of the *Ne Temere* decree of Pius X (1835–1914), who was later canonised. Papal decrees are usually labelled by the first few words of their Latin text and *Ne Temere* ('Lest rashly…') dealt with the knotty problem of marriage between Catholics and members of other religions. The problem had been dealt with less rigour during previous centuries but now the pope reaffirmed what had for many years been Church teaching that such 'mixed' marriages were null and void if solemnised elsewhere than in a Catholic church, and that even then the maimed rites could take place only after a promise that any children would be reared as Catholics. These regulations had already been agreed at the Synod of Thurles (1850), which had been masterminded by the resolute Paul Cullen but, as with many papal pronouncements, they made life for Belfast Catholics more difficult than ever.

The notorious McCann affair (1910) merely confirmed Protestant fears and supplied the Protestant newspapers with splendid copy. A Belfast Catholic, Alexander McCann, who had married a Presbyterian, came to believe that his marriage was null and void and left his wife, taking with him their two children. The rift was believed to have been instigated by his confessor though there was no formal Church statement about the affair. It was a painful case and one that played into the hands of vocal militant Protestants who maintained that all their rights would be taken away from them in the Catholic Church-dominated state that would inevitably follow Home Rule. Only those on the very naïve and extreme edge of anti-Catholicism believed this but it gave the leaders of Unionism, determined to prevent the cataclysm of devolution, ample fodder for their rhetoric.

Though the Dunraven suggestion was shelved with the fall of the

Conservative government of A[rthur] J[ames] Balfour (1848–1930), the northern Unionists were watchful. They knew that devolution was, on paper, at least, part of the Liberal agenda and though it was not part of any King's Speech in the years of plenty it was bound to arise in 1910 when the government needed the 84 parliamentary votes controlled by Redmond.

The Ulster Unionists acquired a new leader on 21 February 1910 – or rather two new leaders, notably dissimilar in appearance and abilities. Edward Carson (1854–1935) – he was knighted in 1900 as solicitor-general in the Conservative government – was brilliant with a stellar career as a barrister behind him and an even more glittering career in politics ahead. He was tall and, because of the set of his strong features, menacing. He was a brilliant if unshowy speaker and was taken to Ulster's bosom as its saviour. Yet in spite of his stage presence he was a man of great uncertainties. His dedication to any accepted cause was absolute and in pursuit of his perceived goals he could be ruthless. This was seen dramatically in his demolition in the witness box of his university friend Oscar Wilde (1854–1900) in his defence of the rabid Marquess of Queensberry (1844–1900) that led to Wilde's arrest and imprisonment. Despite his obvious physical strength he was a persistent hypochondriac and died a disappointed man, having failed to achieve his life's ambition of saving the Union.

His second-in-command, James Craig, was strikingly different in appearance and in abilities. His stolid, almost bucolic, appearance hid a temperament that was imperturbable and brilliant at organisation. His father had joined the offices of Dunville's distillery as a junior clerk and had become a millionaire part-owner by the age of 50. James was the sixth son with seven brothers and one sister, and was sent to school in Edinburgh so that there was no need to lose his Ulster accent. He was colour-blind – a Daltonist – which meant he could not distinguish red from green. Patrick Buckland, one of his biographers, commenting on this, said '…which also meant he could hardly distinguish orange from green!' In fact neither he nor Carson had the least trace of *religious* intolerance; it was just unfortunate that from the Unionist point of view many of their adversaries were also Catholics as well as Home Rulers.

Craig's military experience was acquired during the Second Boer War (1899–1902). He showed great coolness and daring in battle and endurance in captivity, refusing transport with the other officers and marching the 200 miles to the prison camp with the other ranks. Later, having returned to Durban, he helped run the military rail system to which he brought his flair for attention to detail and organisation. When the crisis arrived with the certainty of the passing of a Home Rule bill, Ulster, as Lord Randolph Churchill had foretold, would fight but whether it would also be right would be a matter for the outside world to determine. What became clear in the hurly-burly of those years was that Carson remained an absolute Unionist, fighting with every ounce of his strength to preserve the Act of Union. Craig, however, revealed himself as an avid Home Ruler for *Ulster*, in so far as that nebulous entity could be defined.

A number of things combined to determine the unsatisfactory final shape of political Ireland. One was the support that Unionism had in Britain, in the higher ranks of the army, in the judiciary, in the House of Lords, and among the industrial magnates. Asquith had many talents but he never seemed to summon up the nerve to face down these supporters. As late as 1916, just before his retirement from politics, or really his defeat by Lloyd George, he was unable to prevent General Sir John Maxwell (1859–1929) carrying out his deliberately paced and agonising sequence of executions of the 1916 leaders. He saw that the populace, until then largely dismissive of the Volunteers and the Citizen Army, were being made to support Sinn Féin but his telegrammed instructions were ignored. He may not have been as unaware of the resolution of the Ulster Unionists as Redmond seemed to be. He must have realised that between 1910 and 1912 Protestant Ulster had constituted itself an independent state with its own army and even an already designed coinage.

The army was later known as the Ulster Volunteer Force (UVF). It was created in January 1913 to coordinate the various strands of paramilitary activity that needed to be brought under the control of the leadership, specifically that of Craig, who was able to use the network of Orange lodges that existed in most Ulster towns and villages. When the arms arrived at Larne, Bangor and Donaghadee (from Germany, ironically, considering the date: 24–25 April 1914) in the gun-running organised by F[rederick] H[ugh] Crawford (1861–1952), the authorities as constituted by the RIC and the army turned several blind eyes and the not entirely suitable weapons were spirited away and concealed throughout Protestant Ulster. It was a typical piece of Craig organisation and should have chilled the blood of lesser politicians than Asquith and Redmond. Meanwhile the city with the greatest concentration of population and the place of easy access for demonstrations played its part in the whipping-up of the Protestant exaltation necessary for the ultimate possibility of civil war.

Craig's family home, Craigavon in Strandtown, was the scene on 23 September 1911 of an assembly of 50,000 supporters who heard Carson utter the treasonable and illegal words: 'We must be prepared the morning Home Rule passes, ourselves to become responsible for the government of the Protestant Province of Ulster.' The grounds of Craigavon were extensive, sweeping from the house set on the crest of a hill, where Craig had set up his platform, down to the lough. Even those who could not actually hear what Carson was saying could not but be impressed by his appearance. His confidence in his capacity to fight the Liberal government's betrayal of Ulster was increased by the realisation that more and more retired British army officers were available to train the other ranks.

The following Easter Tuesday, 9 April 1912, Carson and Craig were joined by Andrew Bonar Law (1858–1923), the new leader of the Conservative Party in Westminster, at a mass rally in the Balmoral showgrounds. One hundred thousand men marched in two strands on either side of the platform. The general atmosphere of spectacle was enhanced by a 90-foot flagstaff from which, as the anti-Home Rule resolution was passed, a giant Union Flag, 48 foot by 25 foot, was unfurled. It was believed to be the largest ever woven, and what better source for such an icon than Linenopolis in all its pride! Bonar Law's instinct as a Scot, though born in Canada, was to support his 'kith and kin' in Ulster but the crisis also gave him a political platform, which the Conservative Party needed. He could provide the kind of rhetoric that his listeners needed to hear: 'You have saved yourself by your exertions, and you will save the Empire by your example.'

His statement at a rally on what then could be called without hesitation the 'mainland' at Blenheim Palace in Oxfordshire in July seemed to commit him to the same kind of illegal activity that the UVF proposed to implement: 'I can imagine no length of resistance to which Ulster can go in which I shall not be prepared to support them.' This sort of language sounds now like bluster and was certainly unparliamentary but his listeners found it cheering. Their state of mental exhilaration needed very little reassurance, as a series of rallies beginning in Enniskillen on 12 September and ending in Belfast on Covenant Day, 28 September, was to show.

Aside from gaining political advantage – if the Conservatives had been able to hold an election then they could easily have won – Bonar Law's purpose was to warn of the dissolution of the great empire that could conceivably happen should Ireland gain her independence. The apocalyptic nature of his oratory probably concealed a less gloomy belief. In the first place the devolution offered did not amount to anything like independence. Westminster was to retain control of imperial and foreign affairs, armed forces, currency, security and major taxation. In one respect, however, Bonar Law and others fearful of the erosion of the British Empire were to have their worst fears realised because of the handling of Irish affairs by successive British governments and their security forces. The granting of the limited hegemony guaranteed by the Anglo-Irish Treaty signed on 6 December 1921 led eventually to the declaration of the independent Republic of Ireland on 21 December 1948. More than a year earlier the declaration of India's independence made it clear to the world that the sun was setting at last on the Empire. Protestant Ulster had not saved it by its example. The truth is that all empires eventually crumble but perhaps Ireland, north and south, began the erosion – the south by the aftermath of its war of independence, the north by its provincial detachment from world affairs.

Belfast was to become a capital but not of a country or even a province. Rather it was to hold the government of six carefully chosen counties that would form a political entity constructed to ensure a permanent Unionist majority. This historical outcome may have squared with Craig's ultimate ambition but it displeased Carson and is unlikely to have occurred to those who cheered their fiery speeches.

To the people of the city the years 1912–14 brought drama and, to the Protestant population, it brought a euphoria that was almost pathological. Photographs of Covenant Day are still breathtaking. One taken from behind the statue of Queen Victoria at the front of the City Hall where the main signing took place shows Donegall Square, Donegall Place and Royal Avenue so crowded with men anxious to sign the Solemn League and Covenant that nothing of the pavements or roadways can be seen: 237,368 men signed the document that reeked of seventeenth-century obduracy.[1] It was typical of Carson's big bow-wow style that he should choose for the occasion the name of an agreement made between Scots Presbyterians and the English Parliamentary party in 1643 against Charles I. Its wording, devised by a colleague, Thomas Sinclair, had the kind of biblical resonance that the signatories could recognise and identify with:

> Being convinced in our consciences that Home Rule would be disastrous to the material well-being of Ulster as well as of the whole of Ireland, subversive of our civil and religious freedom, destructive of our citizenship and perilous to the unity of the Empire… we… do hereby pledge ourselves

in solemn Covenant… to stand by one another in defending for ourselves and our children our cherished position of equal citizenship in the United Kingdom and in using all means which may be found necessary to defeat the present conspiracy to set up a Home Rule Parliament…

There was more in this vein but the message was clear: Ulster would fight. Some like Crawford overdid the drama by signing in their own blood but it was unnecessarily melodramatic in the circumstances. The real drama was in the crowds who signed in ink in Derry, Enniskillen, Armagh, as well as in the city. The day passed without any civic trouble, probably because the sheer number of signatories daunted any troublemakers. There had been a riot a fortnight before at a football match in Celtic Park between Belfast Celtic and their old rivals Linfield but the other disturbances and property destruction had been caused by the extremely militant suffragettes. Yet the prospect of civil war must have caused the nationalist population of the city serious concern. They remembered how in the summer of 1912 there had been trouble in the Island when 2,000 Catholics had been expelled by Protestant workers and 300 left the city for good.

The Ulster crisis continued. After the landings in April 1914 the UVF had in its possession a total of 37,000 rifles and carbines and the drilling, no longer illegal since it was by permission of local magistrates, continued with real guns and bullets, instead of the wooden rifles that their opponents mocked. Detailed plans for the running of an independent state were firmly in place. The UVF had ready cavalry, a motorised unit and a specially trained strike force. Plans were in place for them to control roads, bridges and railways. A detailed list of women and children evacuees was drawn up, with priority given to the wives and families of the special strike force, and reception centres prepared for them in England and Scotland. Craig was involved in a scheme to bring in supplies of food from Glasgow in anticipation of a naval blockade. The Curragh incident of 20 March, in which 57 out of 70 officers in the headquarters of the army in Ireland threatened to resign their commissions if they were asked to impose Home Rule against the wishes of Unionists, showed that the Liberal government had little control of the War Office. It is probable, too – at least, so it was believed – that the UVF, through Carson and his contacts with members of the High Command, were given regular reports of all War Office plans for dealing with Ulster.

The Home Rule Bill had its third reading on 25 May 1914 but already Asquith was beginning to consider an amendment that would permit a kind of county opt-out from its terms. Redmond had to advise Asquith not to try to impose Home Rule against the wishes of those who could cause a *coup d'état* within 24 hours, with 24,000 armed and trained men in Belfast alone to set against about 1,000 soldiers and the confused RIC. There was some attempt made by the northern IRB to arm Catholics in vulnerable areas but these were pitifully inadequate against an almost certain city pogrom and attacks in Down, north Armagh and south Antrim. In a rather despairing attempt to reach some kind of agreement, Asquith persuaded George V (1865–1936) to call a meeting in Buckingham Palace on 20 July of all interested parties. He and Lloyd George represented the government, Bonar Law and Lord Lansdowne (1845–1927) the opposition, Carson and Craig the Ulster Unionists, and Redmond and Dillon the Nationalists. The conscientious king said in his introductory (and only) speech that it was to him unthinkable 'that we should be bought to the brink of fratricidal strife upon issues so capable of adjustment as these you are now asked to consider, if handled in a spirit of generous compromise'. Such a compromise was found to be beyond the reach of the meeting. Redmond and Dillon could not understand why so limited a measure of devolution should cause such terrors in Protestant Ulster, showing again their misreading of the psychology of their opponents; Bonar Law and his aristocrat House of Lords leader were there to defend the integrity of the Empire, and the Liberals were desperate for an acceptable solution.

The conference was essentially about the nature of the inevitable partition. Carson was willing to take the gamble of a nine-county Ulster that would have meant a knife-edge majority; Redmond wanted to protect the Nationalists of Derry city and those of Tyrone and Fermanagh. Asquith's suggestion implied the exclusion of the six northeastern counties that in fact later constituted Northern Ireland but neither Carson nor Redmond would accept this. In his report of failure to the Cabinet on 24 July Asquith spoke with some pathos: 'Nothing could have been more amicable in tone or more desperately fruitless in result.'

Already, however, the government had something even more serious to deal with: Austria had sent its ultimatum to Serbia. It declared war four days later, Russia mobilised and Germany, which had waited for the opportunity, declared war on France, using Belgium as a backdoor entrance. On 4 August Britain declared war on Germany and Austria, bound as they were by old alliances. As Churchill wrote in his book *The World Crisis* (1923), 'The parishes of Fermanagh and Tyrone faded back into the mists and squalls of Ireland.' (Funny, how Ireland is always blamed for its weather!)

There was a sense of relief, for all honourable men, it was felt, would recognise and respond to the cataclysm that threatened European civilisation. Though the Home Rule Bill became law on 18 September it was accompanied on Asquith's instructions by a bill suspending its operation until the end of the war. Even the diplomats whose rigidity and incompetence had caused the outbreak believed in the current phrase that 'it would all be over by Christmas'. The Irish-born Lord Kitchener (1850–1916) was made Secretary for War almost immediately and, aware of the depleted state of what the Kaiser William II (1859–1941), one of the few leaders who actually wanted war, called the 'contemptible little army', set about a massive recruiting campaign. He turned to Carson, although the two men could not abide each other, and asked for the UVF. Carson and Craig immediately delivered 35,000 men who were to form the 36th (Ulster) Division. Craig became quartermaster-general of the Ulster Division and Carson served not very successfully in various posts in the war administration. It was typical of him that once he had promised his men to Kitchener he should personally visit Moss Bros, the outfitters, off the Strand in London, and order 10,000 uniforms.

In Belfast the centre of UVF operations had been the Old Town Hall in Victoria Street, intended as headquarters in the expected civil war, and the recruiting officers took over another building close by. The men went from the Old Town Hall after authentication and were fitted out with complete uniforms at the recruitment building. About one third of the Ulster Division was made up of Belfast citizens and when they marched away on 8 May 1915 the city was decorated all over and cheering crowds thronged the streets.

The battle that they had trained for and eagerly awaited took place on 1 July 1916 at the Ancre, a tributary of the Somme. After two days, 5,500 of them had been killed, some of them wearing Orange collarettes as they marched into battle. As the dire casualty lists became known in the city, the UVF unit given after the name of each victim fell silent. There were no Twelfth of July processions; instead Belfast people standing in pouring rain kept a bleak five minutes silence. Their courage and dedication to king and empire was beyond question, but later generations look back on the battle, that ceased only when in November the weather made continuation impossible, as a monstrous and inexcusable sacrifice of young men. The Ulster Division showed by its demeanour and intrepidity just how formidable a foe they would have made in a civil war fought on their home ground.

In all, 50,000 Irish soldiers died in this so-called 'Great' War, at least half of them Catholics/Nationalists. Of these 4,000 joined in Belfast in 1915 and, like the UVF, were all volunteers.[2] At the beginning of the war Redmond had urged Irishmen to join his National Volunteers who, acting as a defensive force, could release regulars stationed in Ireland to fight in the trenches. Others marching to a different drummer found it necessary to form their own Irish

Volunteers and it was these who were accused of 'stabbing their kith and kin in the back' by rising on 24 April 1916, eleven weeks before the Somme, and changed Irish politics utterly. The Easter Rising dismayed nearly all Nationalist leaders, even Eóin MacNeill, the founder of these alternative Volunteers. Griffithites like Robert Lynd and Tom Kettle (1880–1916), the leading Nationalist MP, were greatly upset, and it may well have shortened Redmond's life.[3]

It was the Easter Rising that finally persuaded Lloyd George of the necessity of exclusion of a workable number of counties. Though not in use then, the acronym 'Fatlad' – or 'Fatdad' if, as a Nationalist, one couldn't bear to call the northwest county Londonderry – stood for the exclusion zone.[4] The Nationalists of Fermanagh, Tyrone and Derry city were going to be included against their will in the strange political creation, Northern Ireland, and the Unionists of Monaghan, Cavan and Donegal were excluded from that state with permanent Protestant hegemony and compelled to live as a minority in the new Free State. Even 'Wee Joe' was persuaded that the imposition of a solution was better than a civil war in which Catholics, almost totally without weaponry, would have stood no chance against the UVF and a British army now hostile because of the events of Easter Week.

The war lurched murderously on. Those at home in Belfast unwillingly learned the names of such places as St Omer, Messines, St Julien and Ypres as more and more of their young men died. The welfare of the Ulster Division continued to concern the people left behind. The movement had had great support in the few years before the war and continued during hostilities. A characteristic of the propaganda of both sides in these years was the use of postcards. These were published mainly in Belfast but also in Dungannon and across the Irish Sea. The more effective examples supported Ulster. One headed 'Ulster 1914' and captioned 'Deserted! Well – I can stand alone,' showed what de Valera might have called a 'comely Ulster maiden' holding a smuggled rifle while a tousled Union flag fluttered behind her. Another had a frustrated Redmond blocked by

Ulster's bloody red hand beneath the words: 'Stand back Redmond. Your bill may pass parliament but it will not pass Ulster.' Even the famous Donald McGill (Fraser Gould) (1875–1962), cherished for his risqué seaside postcards, contributed one showing a Nationalist in stage-Irish costume kissing a pretty Unionist lass under the words 'Home Rule' done in green, with the mildly naughty caption, 'An Act of Union which satisfies both parties.' One of the contributing artists was later to be famous as the best portrayer of the streets of Belfast and its people in the twentieth century. This was William Conor (1881–1968) – he explained the unusual spelling of his name by claiming he could never make n's meet – and his card showing helmeted soldiers of the Ulster Division, charging with fixed bayonets 'at Thiepval, 1st July 1916' sold in its thousands. The proceeds of this and other Ulster Division cards by Conor went to aid the UVF Hospital for Sick and Wounded Soldiers and Sailors.

The war surprised everybody by being over before the Christmas of 1918 and, in Churchill's famous words, delivered in the House of Commons on 16 February 1922, in spite of the deluge that had overcome the world, '…as the waters fall short, we see the dreary steeples of Fermanagh and Tyrone emerging once again'.

A rough beast, at least from the point of view of Ulster Nationalists, was slouching towards Belfast to be born and it was going to be a pretty bloody confinement. The war years, apart from the terrible casualty figures, had not been too bad in the city. The shipyards were going full blast with some Catholics employed to replace the many volunteers. Harland & Wolff built 400,000 tons of merchant and naval shipping and even the 'wee yard' of Workman Clark produced 260,000 tons. Belfast supplied half of the Royal Navy's ropes and 90 million yards of aeroplane fabric. Pirrie, anxious as ever to diversify, began to build planes. Harry Ferguson (1884–1960) – among other things, an active gun-runner for the UVF – had built and flown Ireland's first plane but his main contribution to the 'Grow More Food' wartime campaign was the invention of a plough that could be mounted on a tractor, thus doing an onerous and tedious job much more quickly. He later invented a tractor with the mounted implements hydraulically controlled and in 1939 joined forces with Henry Ford (1865–1947) in a famous 'handshake' agreement to build and market the Fordson tractor.

Ferguson was typical of Belfast men of talent, who, intensely proud of the city and its achievements, could see no advantage for it under Home Rule. Like many others of his townsmen he was prepared to risk his life for the perceived advantages of maintaining the union with Britain. Proud of their virtues of honesty, industry, practicality, they could not understand Nationalists looking to an older Irish history that they could not share. Their allegiance and commitment were ironically to a Britain that scarcely understood them, unable even to distinguish them from the older Irish they regarded as adversaries. Unlike the Sinn Féin traitors in the rest of the country they had volunteered to fight the Germans because their leaders had advised it and now that that struggle was over they were ready for the older one again. The mandate given by the success of Sinn Féin in the post-war general election (December 1918), the first under universal adult male suffrage, indicated that the party was not going to settle for the limited devolution offered by the 1914 act. They won 73 of a total of 105 Irish seats, while the old Redmondites got no more than six; 'Wee Joe', however, defeated de Valera in West Belfast.

The following year saw the start of what later became known as the 'Tan War' and the Irish Republican Army (IRA), the military wing of Sinn Féin, engaged in a campaign of violence against the RIC, their supplementary force, the 'Black and Tans', made up of British ex-soldiers, and the even more feared and detested 'Auxies', the auxiliary force of 1,900 demobilised British army officers who earned a lasting reputation for brutality and drunkenness. Most of the violence took place in the south and west of Ireland and there was less activity in the northeast. The towns of Dublin, Cork,

Limerick and Galway were subject to attacks but a considerable part of the IRA campaign was in the counties of Munster. County Cork (including the city) saw 50 attacks, Tipperary 29, Kerry 20, and Limerick 14. The first RIC fatality in Belfast was Constable Thomas Leonard, who was on patrol at Broadway on the Falls Road, and was shot on 25 September 1920. As the civil war in Ulster intensified the IRA could appear in a defensive light to the significantly outnumbered Catholics.

In 1919 the city was more concerned with a strike by Belfast workers in the shipyards, the engineering works and the city's gasyards and electricity stations. The workers were no longer prepared to tolerate the 54-hour wartime working week and demanded its reduction to 44 hours. Children, as they played in the streets, repeated the strikers' mantra: 'We'll work no more till we get the forty-four.' The strike began on 25 January and affected more than 40 firms. Its effect was rather that of a small-scale general stoppage. There were no trams or street lights and, with no gas, meals had to cooked on coal-fired ranges or open fires. Most of the strikers were Protestant – they were the ones with the jobs – but in spite of the *Belfast News Letter* (in reduced size because of lack of power, and using blackleg labour) thundering that the strike was aiding Sinn Féin, the action was simply for better conditions. On 14 February, when the strike was three weeks old, the troops were ordered to take over the utilities, but six days later, the strikers settled for a 47-hour week. Over the next three years the workers were to play an even more vigorous role, not for improvement in pay and conditions, and one that showed only partial working-class solidarity.

10

Capital City

LLOYD GEORGE HAD BEEN KEEN TO grant Home Rule in 1916 with some exclusion for the Ulster counties. Though urged to do so by Asquith he was balked in this by Walter Long (1854–1924), once chief secretary and now a senior Unionist. He was chairman of the Irish Situation Committee that reported on 4 November 1919 and its findings became the basis for the (Better) Government of Ireland Act. It was introduced to parliament on 25 February 1920 and became law on 23 December. It set up two parliaments in Ireland, one to rule six carefully selected counties that would permanently preserve Unionist ascendancy, the other to rule the 26 counties of Saorstat Éireann that had been granted dominion status. Lloyd George and indeed Carson had hoped that the basis for the new separate state within the United Kingdom would be the historical nine-county province of Ulster but Craig would not risk the possibility of a future Nationalist majority voting Northern Ireland out of existence again. Carson had argued earlier for a state composed of the four 'safe' Unionist counties of Londonderry, Antrim, Down and Armagh, which had 'a population greater than New Zealand or Newfoundland' but was eventually persuaded that the area was too small.

Though the act was not put into force until 3 May 1921, already by early 1920 the IRA had begun a peripheral campaign in the North, capturing the Shantonagh barracks in Monaghan and establishing a presence in the city. A pattern of intimidation and lethal violence began to emerge. At the various 'fields' where Orangemen assembled on 12 July the brethren were harangued and magisterially reassured that they would be protected from 'the machinations of Sinn Féin'. The same kind of emotional rhetoric that had characterised the years 1912 to 1914 was recklessly used by such speakers as Carson addressing the main demonstration at Finaghy: '...we will take the matter into our own hands. We will reorganise.'

In the pre-war years the enemy was vague, centred mainly on the Liberal administration, with Catholics only a secondary consideration. Now in default of a more obvious adversary all Catholics, no matter what their personal politics, were regarded as Sinn Féin supporters, the heirs of the back-stabbers of 1916. Ulster anticipated McLuhanism in becoming a provincial village. Trouble in Derry was experienced as happening in the next street. There had been trouble in the Maiden City all summer and it had become clear that two illegal organisations had been engaged in a kind of urban civil war with, as ever, civilians caught in the crossfire. The UVF had risen again from the ashes of the trenches, now with war experience, and ready to pass on military skills to eager young recruits. When Carson had promised, 'We will reorganise,' he may not have had a specific plan in mind but it seems that Craig had.

The problem of dealing with the illegal UVF was solved with ease by reconstituting them as members of three special constabularies (the Ulster Special Constabulary, or USC). Of these the most significant were the B-Specials, a part-time, unpaid force with UVF officers who remained a constant threat to Catholics until its forced disbandment in 1970.[1] Because of the influence that Balfour and to a lesser extent the ailing Bonar Law, always friends of Unionism, still had in the British ruling coalition Ulster and its leaders were being given their head. Furthermore the ever more intense IRA campaign made Craig and his men seem models of rectitude and good government. 'Wee Joe' had fought valiantly in the Commons to prevent this licensed force. As he accused: 'The Chief Secretary is going to arm pogromists to murder Catholics.' The trouble in Derry was over by August, the IRA routed not by the UVF or the army but by the Church. In Belfast it continued sporadically for two more years.

No census was taken in 1921, mostly for security reasons, but also because of confusion about who had the authority to gather the information. The 1911 figures show that out of a total population of 386,947 in the city, 93,243 were Catholic, a percentage of 24.1. By the time that the next census figures, those of 1926, were collated the urban population was 415,151 with 95,682 of these Catholic, the percentage having dropped a point. This contrasts with 1861 when Catholics formed a third of the 119,393 citizens. The percentage for the next 50 years was to hover just below a quarter, proof that there was no conspiracy, as many believed, by Catholics to flood the Protestant city.

Between July 1920 and June 1922 a total of 455 citizens died by violent means. Of these, 267 were Catholic and 37 were members of the security forces. The Catholic figure should be read with this consideration, that they formed less than a quarter of the city's population. Unquestionably some of the killings were done by men in the black uniform of the B-Specials, sometimes with spurious logic as reprisals for injury to their own force. Probably the most horrific single incident was that involving the family of a wealthy Catholic publican, Owen McMahon. Early on the morning of 24 March 1922 a group of armed men broke into the McMahon house in Kinnaird Terrace beside St Malachy's College in the lower Antrim Road and dragged the male members of the household out of bed. McMahon, his five sons, one aged fifteen and a half, and Edward McKinney, a bartender, were lined up against the living room wall and shot. Four died immediately, the others the following day. The youngest of the family, aged six and a half, escaped by creeping under the sofa and, though two shots were aimed at it, he survived. One other son, John McMahon, aged 21, survived and reported from his hospital bed that though the killers wore RIC uniforms, he suspected that they were B-Specials. He added that they spoke with strong Belfast accents. It is firmly believed that JW Nixon, a district inspector of the RIC, was in charge of the firing party. Nothing was ever proved and no one brought to justice. Nixon was dismissed from the RUC in 1924 for extremism but remained as a thorn in the flesh of the Stormont government as an Independent Unionist for Woodvale (1929–49).

The McMahon killings remain part of the dark history of sectarian Belfast still known as the 'pogrom', still mentioned with a mixture of rage and awe.[2] The immediate cause of the atrocity may have been the killing by the IRA of two B-Specials at 12.15pm the previous afternoon in the city. William Chermside from Portaferry in the Ards peninsula and Thomas Cunningham from Cavan were on patrol on Victoria Street and had just turned into May Street when they were shot in the back by the IRA. They were the twenty-fourth and twenty-fifth fatalities since the formation of the special constabularies in November 1920, and 19 more were to be killed before the end of 1922. The last police officer to die in these years was Special Constable Samuel Hayes, who was shot in a pub in the Newtownards Road, Belfast, on 5 August 1922.

The truce in the Tan War came into effect on 11 July 1921 and the RIC were no longer regarded as necessary targets in the 26 counties that would form the Free State after the signing of the Treaty. The Royal Ulster Constabulary (RUC) replaced the RIC on 1 June 1922, retaining a large proportion of the original force. Their assumption of control coincides almost with the beginning of the Civil War and though they were less likely to be targets for the IRA, both wings, Treatyites and Anti-Treatyites alike, continued to attack them.

Some violence was inevitable, especially in the city with the largest concentration of Catholics anywhere in the province and the proximity of hostile areas. The prevailing atmosphere was one of fear, all the more disturbing since the causes were imprecise. Protestants had, in fact, little to fear. They had won all the battles and were sure they had won the war. A sense of unease and indeed unreality still pervaded their ranks. Some of them were a little bit defensive about the condition of their Catholic neighbours and, while describing them with different levels of vituperation, usually would admit to exceptions, personal acquaintances who were 'really very decent people'. This was especially true among middle-class Protestants who, though benefiting from a near exclusive access to public sector jobs and the higher levels of professional appointment, were in fact on fairly intimate terms with their Catholic fellows: successful businessmen, doctors, lawyers, teachers and even priests.

Protestant fears were set in the cement of a threatened rule by Rome. For many this was *faux-naif*; the pervasiveness of Church influence among its flocks was in matters not so much of politics or commerce but of morality. In a sense Belfast Protestants were as much ruled by Canterbury and Assembly's College as Catholics were by Rome. In later years, as the Church seemed to strengthen its grip on the Free State in matters of birth control, divorce and censorship, northern Protestants loudly demonstrated their relief in their freedom from such control. Yet in the years of the setting up of the Northern Ireland state there was not that much difference in moral standards and practice between the two faiths.

There was no longer any real threat of 'Rome rule' since Protestants had already achieved a much greater amount of Home Rule than that offered to the South. They did dread that things might somehow change back and so were adamant about stifling any chance of the relinquishing of the freedoms they felt they had won. A stronger fear still was that of an IRA campaign that might have the same intensity as the one that raged in the South from January 1919 till July 1922 and contrive the same kind of separatist victory. In this matter the attitude and actions of the first Dáil, set up in 1919, towards the North were at best tactically unsound and at worst inept. The mishandling of relations was based partly upon Sinn Féin's congenital misreading of the Northern situation and its need to concentrate upon its waging of the Anglo-Irish war. Urged on largely by Michael Collins (1890–1922), Sinn Féin felt that some response to the pogrom of the summer of 1920 was essential.

Trouble had begun on 21 July, the first day back at work after the 'Twelfth', at which Carson and other Unionist leaders practically urged their followers to deal with 'disloyal workers' themselves. There was an understandable resentment that many Catholics who had wisely remained non-combatant had been taken on in the large industries at full production because of the needs of war to fill the places left vacant by the volunteers of the Ulster Division. Now was the chance to get rid of them and so they were expelled violently from the 'wee yard' of Workman Clark, their expulsion hastened by 'Belfast confetti', rivets and bolts carried for the purpose by 'loyal' apprentices. They invaded Harland & Wolff's yard causing some of the Catholics to have to swim ashore.

The term 'disloyal' was mainly applied to Catholics but also included in the expulsions were 'socialists', also anathema. They were driven out from other large firms like Mackie's, and the Sirocco Engineering Works. In the rioting that followed seven Catholics and six Protestants died violently.

There was further trouble in August with violent confrontations in Ballymacarrett when St Matthew's Catholic Church was attacked, and the Marrowbone Lane, a tiny Catholic enclave known locally as the 'Bone', between the Crumlin Road and the Oldpark Road in north Belfast. The deadly score for that August was 22 dead, 400 Catholics driven from their homes. Just as the month ended the army, visibly on the side of Protestants, imposed a curfew that was to remain in force for two years. People were required to stay indoors 'between the hours of 10.30pm and 5am'. Places of entertainment were to close and trams stop running at 9.30. If its purpose was to restore public order it failed in the short term. The death tally for

September was five soldiers, two policemen, 35 Catholics and 32 Protestants.

The Dáil's response to the events of the summer was a call on 6 August for a boycott of banking and insurance originating in Belfast. It soon spread to all goods from Belfast and was prosecuted by the IRA with much vigour and little commonsense, attacking goods trains with whiskey and tobacco cargoes, and raiding shops in Dublin selling Belfast goods. Like most attempts to aid the Belfast Catholic it failed miserably; no expelled Catholics were reinstated and its secondary purpose of illustrating the kind of economic hardship that a severed Northern Ireland should suffer merely stiffened Unionist resistance and made more palpable the reality of partition.

In spite of the Conservative/Unionist elements in Lloyd George's coalition government he was forced to insist on meetings between Craig and Collins in January and March 1922. They promised much but achieved little. Catholics were not reinstated and Collins set up an IRA 'City Guard' which simply exacerbated the condition of the already hard-pressed Catholics. The McMahon killings had followed hard upon the deaths of Chermside and Cunningham in March 1922 and an IRA attack on a train carrying a USC party, in which four officers were killed on 11 February, resulted in the deaths of three utterly innocent Belfast Catholics – Bernard McKenna, William Spallen and Joseph Walsh – who were shot in their beds in Arnon Street, in the Catholic area of Carrick Hill by a USC patrol. This was 'answered' the next day by the killing, probably by the City Guard, of three Protestants in a barrel works in Little Patrick Street.

Another IRA raid, in fact a botched attempt to steal armoured cars and arms from Musgrave Barracks on 18 May, was answered by the USC's killing 15 Catholics in the Lower Falls. The catalogue of horrors continued until a kind of exhausted peace fell upon the beleaguered city as the summer ended. One cause was the almost total disaffection between the Catholic population and the City Guard. Even the *Irish News*, the voice of northern Nationalism since 1891, called upon the

IRA to stop their senseless campaign since it was really to the ultimate disadvantage and danger of Catholics. The beginning of the Civil War in July 1922 split the northern battalions and though there was some continuity of campaign by both Treatyites and 'diehards', as they were called, a kind of peace came with faltering steps.

Even allowing for Protestant fears of loss of liberty and future rule from Dublin, and the visceral need for reprisal for death of colleagues, much of the violence against Catholics, usually in the well-designated Catholic districts of Falls-Smithfield, New Lodge, the Markets, Ardoyne, Short Strand, Dock and Greencastle, was punitive, rooted in religious hatred. The situation slowly began to improve by 1923 with the end of activity by the IRA and the internment of its leaders. A notorious murder gang known as the United Protestant League that had been responsible for many mindless Catholic deaths had been assimilated into the USC. Lloyd George had agreed to the establishment of the force partly because of Craig's usual threat of resignation when he made a demand and because he felt that some structured body like the USC was more controllable than freelance anti-Catholic vigilantes. The arrest of members of a group called the Ulster Protestant Association, accused of murdering Catholics in the late summer and autumn of 1922, did something to relieve the bitter sense of injustice felt by the war-weary Catholics of the city.

In spite of two years of almost continuous civil war some political progress, in Unionists' eyes, had been made. Craig called a general election on 24 May 1921 and was pleased but not surprised that Unionists had won 40 seats, with Sinn Féin six and the rump of the Irish Party six. Neither of these Nationalist parties was, probably wisely, going to give formal recognition to the new ruling party for Northern Ireland. This Unionist majority was to continue at every election until 24 March 1972 when the Stormont parliament was replaced by direct rule under a secretary of state.

By now Craig was a rather weary 50-year-old with a sense that his life's ambition, that of creating Protestant Ulster and 'saving' it from the evil domination of Dublin – or the Vatican – had already been achieved. Yet he knew that more had to be done to safeguard its future. With admirable resolution he had his cabinet chosen by the end of May, a set of worthy men not unlike their prime minister, conscientious, hardworking, possessing of very safe pairs of hands. There were no high fliers but no extremists, with the exception of his Minister of Home Affairs, Sir (since 1921) Dawson Bates. His Civil Authorities (Special Powers) Bill became law on 7 April 1922 and gave draconian powers to the RUC and USC. Acting in the name of the Minister of Home Affairs they could detain without trial, proscribe organisations and ban or reroute parades and marches. It was a tenable response to the actual civil war of the time, though its actions continued to face adamantly in one direction. It was renewed each year, long after the conditions that bred it had passed, until 1933 when it was made permanent. It is believed to have been the envy of the white supremacists in South Africa in the days of apartheid.

The full vigour of its use was demonstrated in 1922 when, following the shooting of WJ Twaddell MP on 22 May on his way to his outfitters shop in Belfast, Bates' Special Powers arrested 350 'known' members of the Northern IRA and interned them in the wooden prison hulk *Argenta* anchored in Larne Lough. Conditions were appalling: the internees were kept in cages, 40 foot by 20 foot by 8 foot, each holding up to 50 people. Tuberculosis and pneumonia were rife and malnutrition was common because of the rotten food.

The action did have the desired effect of weakening the IRA campaign and though the dangerous curfew persisted a deadly peace settled on the city. Craig had reason to feel satisfied but he had one more battle to fight. Under the terms of Article 12 of the Anglo-Irish treaty the problem of the North was to be settled by a 'boundary commission' to make the border with the Free State 'conform as closely as possible to the wishes of the population', but the devilish small print insisted that these wishes had to be 'compatible with economic and geographical considerations'. At best, from the Nationalist point of view, County Tyrone, County Fermanagh, Derry City and Newry might be made part of the Free State. This was small comfort to Belfast's 95,000 Catholics who were going to be barely tolerated second-class citizens under a regime that Craig described at a 'Field' in Poyntzpass on 12 July 1932: 'Ours is a Protestant government and I am an Orangeman.' It was indeed too heavily influenced by the Orange Order that was formally anti-Catholic. As Craig admitted – indeed boasted – in a speech at Stormont as late as 24 April 1934: 'I have always said that I am an Orangeman first and a politician and member of this parliament afterwards.'

The Boundary Commission proved as irrelevant as the Unionists hoped it would be. It met for the first time on 24 November 1924 and was chaired by Richard Feetham (1874–1965), a South African judge of whom Craig approved, though he refused to take part. He had threatened in October to resign with a characteristic speech promising to 'place myself, at the disposal of the people, no longer as prime minister but as their chosen leader, to defend any territory which we may consider has been unfairly transferred from under Ulster, Great Britain and the flag of our Empire'. This customary bluster and accompanying threats had become second nature and his instinct told him that there would be no significant changes. His jealous protectiveness was partly sentimental and partly practical. He wanted Londonderry because it was the iconic 'Maiden City' that had withstood gloriously the seventeenth-century siege and he needed Newry and Mourne because of the Silent Valley reservoir, the chief source of the city's water supply. Ramsay MacDonald (1866–1937), then briefly prime minister, had no stomach for engaging with the Unionists, aware from his experiences in the first decade of the century of canvassing in Belfast, just how recalcitrant they could be. Feetham's pronouncement on 1 November, three weeks before the conference began, really ruled out the possibilities of change:

> If the Commission were to make a change in the boundary in order to
> gratify one of a thousand of such inhabitants at the cost of offending the
> other 999 such a proceeding would obviously be unreasonable.

Eóin MacNeill, the Free State delegate, had little heart in the proceedings and when Feetham's decision to retain the western counties along with Derry and Newry was leaked on 7 November 1925 to the *Morning Post*, a paper never a friend of Ireland, he resigned. On 3 December a tripartite agreement signed by Craig, William Cosgrave (1880–1965), the Free State President of the Executive Council (the term Taoiseach did not come into use until 1937), and Stanley Baldwin (1867–1947), again British prime minister, recognised the existing border. Not for the first time Nationalists, north and south, regretted the early death of Michael Collins, who of all the leaders of Sinn Féin had the truest focus on Northern Ireland.

Belfast Catholics had become a subject people. Joseph MacRory, Bishop of Down and Connor (1881–1945), had joined with other Ulster prelates in refusing to cooperate with such government initiatives as the Lynn Committee on education, probably to their disadvantage, but understandable at the time.

Belfast's Nationalist leader was still 'Wee Joe', shaken by the buffeting his people had taken since 1918 and disappointed that they were virtually defenceless. He was not one to give up the struggle. At first he followed the Nationalist Party line of refusing to recognise the Unionist government and boycotting sessions, held usually in the City Hall or Assembly's College. Later the pointlessness of absolute non-attendance oppressed him so much that, after the second general election in Northern Ireland on 3 April 1925, he took his seat. He knew that he could have no influence on the Unionist majority but being an MP gave him access to committees and members of the Civil Service and Corporation officials where he had still some influence. It was the second hard decision he had to make in his career and it had the same negative effect as his acquiescence in the idea of a form of partition on Redmond's insistence. It effectively distanced him from the rest of the party and inflicted endless frustration on him as he battled with his adamantine adversaries.

He was happier at Westminster where he was appreciated for his still boyish charm and known by the whiff of smoke from his expensive cigars. MacDonald offered him a peerage, which he refused, and a gratuity of £20,000 raised by his friends to let him live in comfort went on paying for the hotel in Bangor that gave the mill girls the only holiday they were likely to get. Another feature of his selfless generosity was the organising of summer day trips to Newcastle or Bangor for the children of west Belfast and beyond. The queues for the buses in Dunville Park to take the children to the station were more than a mile long. He arranged for friends to look after them as they ate their two meals and dole out the bags of sweets and fruit. Since it was summer and the children were poor you would have expected them to be barefoot but Wee Joe made sure that each of them was given new shoes. Odder still was the fact that even his political opponents helped defray the expenses of the Devlin excursion. He died on 18 January 1934 and, as his coffin was taken up his beloved Falls, so many people wanted to help carry it that the procession took hours. The headline in the *Irish News* summed up the day when thousands of people of all shades of political and religious persuasion marched at the funeral: 'Ireland United for a Day.'

The first decade of Northern Ireland's existence slowly wound down. Its parliament had been inaugurated by George V, making another sincere if avuncular attempt at diplomacy. On 22 June 1921, in the council room of the City Hall, he spoke with genuine feeling but with no more confidence than on his last statement in Buckingham Palace before the horrors of Armageddon: 'I speak from a full heart when I pray that my coming to Ireland today may prove to be the first step towards an end of strife among her people, whatever their race and creed.' He also hoped it might be 'the prelude to the day in which the Irish people, North and South, under one parliament or two, as those parliaments shall themselves decide, shall work together in common love for Ireland upon the sure foundation of mutual love and respect'. It would take more than 80 years for such an agreement.

In the meantime the potential traitors had to have one further limited power removed from them; Bates had one further betrayal of the terms of the Government of Ireland Act. The proportional representation (PR) system of voting granted as part of the bill had already given Derry its first Catholic mayor since the seventeenth century and shaken the Unionist dominance of Belfast Corporation, reducing its members from 52 to 29. A bill to abolish PR was hustled through Westminster, becoming law in September 1922, sweeping aside the system and restoring the old ward boundaries. Lloyd George had objected but as usual, because of the shaky nature of his coalition with the Conservatives, acquiesced.

The city remained quiet, the two nations – for so it seemed – learning to co-exist. There was some contact, if only socially, among the middle-class but though the population in 1926 – 415,151 – contained 95,682 Catholics, there were no exact racial characteristics like colour or physiognomy (in spite of firmly held beliefs on both sides). The fact that the city was still a collection of linked villages made local identification fairly easy. Names and – even more so – places of education, required by nearly every potential employer, especially in the public sector, gave a fairly close indication but strangers spent an inordinate amount of time trying to discover the political/religious alignment of companions or, to use the current colloquialism, which foot they kicked with. The potential for trouble was always latent but there was less risk in times of relative economic prosperity. The next decade would have to face the results of the world slump and Belfast would again demonstrate its age-old tendency to sectarian violence.

Hungry Thirties; Fiery Forties

AS WH AUDEN'S (1907–73) 'LOW DISHONEST DECADE' began the capital of Northern Ireland continued its worldwide reputation for primacy in industry and savagery in sectarianism. The first feature was changing; the city's most famous industries, the ones that had identified her for a hundred years, were beginning to decline. Belfast had built ships well but there was almost a glut internationally and she had no longer a virtual monopoly in the product. Her liners were still in demand and during the 1920s the two yards produced 9.7 percent of all British tonnage. The *Britannic*, the world's largest liner was the highlight of 1929 and the total output of vessels of all sizes was the greatest in Britain, the record before the Great War. Nineteen thirty-one saw the launch of the *Georgic*, but orders were sparse. Harland & Wolff were able to diversify, making diesel locomotives and rolling stock for railways, including the Belfast & County Down line that was the first electric diesel in these islands. They also made engines for a Middle East oil pipeline and constructed steel frameworks for new buildings. Workman Clark, the 'wee yard', launched its last vessel, the *Acavus*, a tanker, in January 1935. It was the 536th completed since the business began 66 years previously.

The other great ailing industry was linen. The prestige textile had two negative aspects from the manufacturers' point of view: it was expensive and durable. In a popular pasquinade of the 1930s, 'The Ballad of William Bloat', about the murder of a wife and the suicide of the husband, written by Raymond Calvert (1906–59), the murder attempt failed but the suicide was successful: 'For the razor-blade was German made/But the sheet was Irish linen!' As linen lost its popularity, having to yield to the greater convenience of cotton, exports from Ireland dropped from 200,000 square yards in 1913 to 100,000 in 1937. It still had great prestige in America where society dinner tables were regarded as incomplete without an Irish linen tablecloth. The greater ease in laundering cotton in houses without a large domestic staff spelled the end of its prestige as the fabric of choice for handkerchiefs, nightwear and even undergarments. It was also one of the victims of the world slump that followed in the wake of the Wall Street crash of 23 October 1929. The few who had retained some money in America were ill-disposed to spend it on luxury items like linen.

Tobacco, perhaps not surprisingly, did better. Gallaher's became a public company in 1928 exporting 4,000 tons in 1930 and 10,000 in 1938. Gallaher's 'Blue' cigarettes were still smoked heavily in Belfast, often preferred to Player's or Will's, though Gallaher's small cigarettes, packaged as Park Drive, were much more popular in England. In Belfast the other gasper, Will's Wild Woodbine, outsold any other brand. The 3,000 workers, mostly women, employed in the giant York Street plant were uninterruptedly employed during the Great Depression, as were the rope workers, and Belfast's other, perhaps unlikely, export staple – soft drinks – continued to flourish.

There was great suffering among the poorer people as unemployment grew. The new regime made little attempt to do anything about slum clearance or the building of public housing. There is nothing quite so productive of lethargy and stifling of social conscience as a certainty of one-party government. In 1931 and 1932, the worst years of the depression, in the city there were more than 50,000 unemployed. Though Catholics made up 23 percent of the population as a whole, the percentage unemployed was much greater since Protestants were favoured in most spheres of industry.

The social legislation of the pre-war Liberal government helped mitigate some of the hardships. There was some entitlement for unemployment benefit for those who had been in work and stamped their cards. Even so these best off were only entitled to 26 weeks' dole. After that there was the misery of outdoor relief, made deliberately offensive by the Board of Guardians who supervised its workings. The name of the chairman of the board in 1928, Lily Coleman, has lived on in infamy for her remark, referring to large families, that if the poor made the same effort at finding a job as they did under the blankets there would be less of a problem. Though hers is the name best remembered she spoke for the greater majority of the board. Another complained that 60 percent of the applicants 'are Roman Catholics from a particular quarter of the city'.

The board's main priority was not welfare but how to minimise the burden on the ratepayers. In 1927 it decided to stop outdoor relief to anyone who had been in receipt of help for more than a year. In effect this meant that the 1,097 deprived of aid had either to enter the hated workhouse or go hungry. Not that the relief could be regarded as in any sense generous. Belfast had the lowest grants of any British industrialised area in spite of the pride the members of the board took in being guardians of a city in the kingdom. A man with a wife and one child each week received in Manchester 21 shillings (105 pence), in Liverpool 23 shillings (115 pence), in Bradford 26 shillings (130 pence), and in Nottingham 27 shillings (135 pence). In these cities an additional allowance was made for rent. In Belfast such an essentially uncharacteristic family got twelve shillings (60 pence) with no rent allowance. I have given the present-day equivalent of the amounts but their purchasing power was, of course, greater than that of today's values.

The mean-spiritedness extended beyond simple parsimony. The

board's inspectors had full power to make sure that all savings were exhausted before aid, often in the form of grocery chits, was granted. The means test and the domestic intrusion were humiliating and were borne only because the hunger was real. Some were required to sell carpets and furniture. Single people got nothing and even the recipients had to take part in heavy labouring work for which many were physically unfit.

It is worth remembering that local charities, those associated with the Churches and other independent institutions like Toc H and SVP, were active in what was essentially hunger relief. In 1932 the latter provided £12,000 compared with the board's £7,000. Protest marches were organised with little effect. Then on 3 October 1932, during the depths of the depression, a strike was organised by the Belfast Trades Council, the secretary of which, Betty Sinclair (1900–71), was to have a long career in public affairs in the city. A torchlit procession from the Labour Exchange in Frederick Street to the Custom House attracted 30,000 people. Next day 7,000 accompanied a delegation to the Workhouse. When these peaceful demonstrations had no effect rioting broke out in both the Falls and the Shankill. At once the Special Powers Act swung into force and all marches were banned. On Tuesday, 11 October the RUC almost instinctively chose to face the rioters in the Catholic area, shooting two men, one a Catholic from Smithfield, the other a Protestant flower seller. Word reached the Shankill and unbelievably the people came out in sympathy, attacking the police with equal ferocity.

The next night trouble began in York Street and one man was killed and 30 injured. Even the sluggish Northern Ireland Cabinet could not face such combined, unsectarian protest. They summoned the Board of Guardians to appear before them on 13 October. Unmoved by appeals from all the churches, including special letters from Daniel Mageean (1882–1962), the Catholic bishop, and John Frederick MacNeice (1866–1942), the Church of Ireland bishop and father of the poet, Louis, and complaints even from the city council, they had no alternative but to yield to the government's demand. On 14 October new relief rates were announced: a couple was given £1 and those with children put on a sliding scale from 24 to a maximum of 32 shillings. The next day thousands of people, Catholics and Protestants, led by Tom Mann, the head of the Trades Union Congress (TUC), attended the funeral of Samuel Baxter, the flower seller who had been shot on the Tuesday. It was a mighty victory and one that seemed to herald a new era of working-class solidarity. Such an idea was unthinkable and required action, covert if necessary.

An already existing body, the Ulster Protestant League (UPL), seemed the best source of the desirable disunity. Their policy, expressed here in an unusually restrained form, was 'neither to talk nor walk with, neither to buy nor sell, borrow nor lend, take nor give, or to have any dealings at all with them, nor for employers to employ them, nor employees to work with them'. Some gauge of their extremism may be made from their demanding of Bates to resign as being too soft with 'disloyalists'. They even wanted dismissal of police officers with 'names like Murphy and Flanagan'. It was well that the League was not active when Terence O'Neill (1914–90) became prime minister.

A number of things increased Protestant fears, if indeed there were fears, and not rooted in instinctive hatred. The prospect of the notorious rebel Eamon de Valera as President of the Executive Council of the Free State and the new chairman of the League of Nations was hard to swallow though it was UPL policy to ignore the 'State' as much as possible. The International Eucharistic Congress held in Dublin (22–26 June) could not be ignored, especially when so many Belfast Catholics managed to get to Dublin for the ceremonies. The trains and buses that brought them home were attacked at Banbridge, Lurgan, Portadown and Lisburn. The event, perhaps a little triumphalist, though this was understandable, gave the city's Catholics a new sense of identity as members of an international Church.

The euphoria of the victory over the Board of Guardians was soon dispersed and sectarian watchfulness returned. Members of the government were essentially middle-aged and middle-class but they depended on working-class support and that was obtained by reassuringly sectarian speeches, usually during the marching season at the various 'fields'. On 21 March 1934 Craig (Viscount Craigavon since 1927) refused to repudiate Basil Brooke's call to Derry Unionists the previous night not to employ Catholics, '99% of whom are disloyal'. Speaking in Stormont in the magnificent parliament buildings that had been opened on 16 November 1932 by the Prince of Wales, with his usual heavy imperturbability, he said, 'There is not one of my colleagues who does not entirely agree with him, and I would not ask him to withdraw one word he said.' It was on 24 April, a month later, that he made his notorious 'Orangeman first' speech. Working-class Protestants were being drawn back into the fold and their brief flirtation with Communists like Betty Sinclair forgiven.

Belfast, as we have seen, was no stranger to sectarian violence. In the nineteenth century the usual flashpoint was Durham Street, the boundary between the Pound and Sandy Row. In the first serious outbreak in Northern Ireland the battleground was the warren of mixed-religion streets on both sides of York Street, the city's chief exit route to the north. There were rumblings of discontent in 1933, including the murder of Dan O'Boyle, a Catholic publican there, and in 1934 there were two days of rioting.

In 1935 George V celebrated the silver jubilee of his coronation and his son the Duke of Gloucester (1900–74) came to Belfast to represent him. The visit meant as much to Belfast Protestants as the Eucharistic Congress did to Catholics. Whatever they might feel about individual governments their fondness for royalty was unalloyed. When Catholics refused to join in the celebrations it was seen as further proof of their disloyalty. The visit in May had a touch of the Twelfth about it and there were riots and attacks in Catholic areas, including Willowfield in east Belfast, near the site of the almost completed church of St Anthony. Tension continued to grow during the early summer. An outbreak of shooting in York Street, in spite of the ten o'clock curfew, caused even the granitic Bates to ban, on the advice of Sir Charles Wickham, the Inspector-General of the RUC, all marches in the city. The response from Sir Joseph Davison, the Orange Grand Master, was the shocking but not unexpected statement: 'You may be certain that on the Twelfth of July the Orangemen will be marching throughout Northern Ireland.' An illegal Orange parade took place on 23 June but though the police took names no further action was taken. Four days later Bates rescinded his own order, told to do so by Craigavon, who knew better than to interfere then with Orangemen in their marching season. He was due to leave for one of his increasingly frequent holidays on 17 July. As the Twelfth drew closer many responsible church leaders, including Bishop Mageean and Bishop MacNeice, again appealed for peace.

Trouble began in the Catholic Lancaster Street that ran from York Street to North Queen Street as the marchers were returning from the 'field'. Historians have had difficulty in determining the exact detonator but the *Irish News* of 13 July suggested it was the result of 'a trivial incident'. The riots, involving guns and paving stones, lasted all night and by morning two Protestants and two Catholics were dead and 14 others seriously injured.

The next day an Orange band from Scotland, known as the 'Billy Boys', marched into the Catholic warren of streets east of York Street, accompanied by a crowd, many of whom were not from the area. Fifty-six Catholic houses in six streets were wrecked and burned. The army were mobilised and the sound of machine guns was heard until 4am when it was discovered that two Protestant men had been shot dead.

Later that Sunday trouble spread to the Old Lodge area between the lower ends of the Shankill and Crumlin Roads, where over the next few days Protestant mobs evicted Catholic families. Funerals of victims (often of snipers) caused further rioting and it was not until the following Sunday, 21 July, that the shooting stopped. The final toll was seven Protestants (one killed by his own side as pro-Catholic) and three Catholics. Fifty-five Catholics and 28 Protestants were seriously injured. According to parish records 2,241 Catholics had been driven out from 430 houses. The chief motivation seems to have been to expel Catholics from districts once considered *echt*-Protestant. Typical of the cleansing was the 'Village', the district between Tates Avenue and the Donegall Road, where the evictions were carried out by former neighbours.

One extra cause of the evictions, apart from the usual suspects, was the news that Catholic refugees had occupied a private building venture not yet complete at Glenard, near the Catholic mill quarter of Ardoyne but intended as a 'Protestant' estate by the building speculator, W McKibbin. Sixty Protestant families already in residence fled on 15 July in spite of being asked to stay by a Catholic resettlement committee. The pied piper for this population move was Tommy Geehan, the Communist who with Betty Sinclair had organised the Outdoor Relief strike three years earlier. His involvement sent alarm signals to the Catholic Church and Bishop Mageean bought 48 units to house some of the dispossessed. Glenard eventually accommodated 1,100 Catholic refugees. By 1938 it was regarded as part of Ardoyne and caused a demographic and political shift as it was no longer a safe Unionist seat. There were the usual mutual recriminations as to the causes of this most serious outbreak of public disorder in the lifetime of the new regime. It was not handled well but demands for a commission to investigate the causes were refused by Westminster.

Craigavon was essentially an ill man and his cabinet colleagues were lacking in both energy and talent. Their system, if it may be dignified by that word, was to leave things to the excellent Civil Service, in the senior ranks of which, of course, there were no Catholics, keeping the large Unionist majority happy with the summer speeches that proved their supremacy. Peace descended and sectarian attitudes hardened on both sides. The prevailing mindset, at least among the working classes, was that of two alien species with separate beliefs and to some extent separate cultures. Inevitably the Protestants maintained the siege mentality that had sustained them since the arrival of Catholics in the nineteenth century. They tended to look inwards, viewing social changes with suspicion; Catholics with, in 1937, a total population of 104,372, (23.8 percent of the total) could at least draw on fraternal links with the rest of Ireland, called no longer the Free State but Éire after de Valera's constitutional amendment.[1]

While Protestants read the *Belfast News Letter*, *Northern Whig* and the *Belfast Telegraph*, Catholics were faithful to the *Irish News*. This rational dedication to a purely constitutional paper gave proof, as if it were needed, that they were nearly all non-violent in their politics and hated violence as heartily as the rest of the citizens. Even this statistic must be qualified by the fact that many Protestants bought the *Irish News* because of its sports coverage, which gave the day's fixtures in both horse and dog racing, and nearly everybody took the *Telegraph* because there was no other evening paper and because it gave the early results. Catholics did also buy daily the *Irish Press* and the *Irish Independent*, depending on the buyer's view of the Treaty of 1921.

The fact that Belfast was no longer, and had not been for years, a totally Protestant city, as God intended, continued to rankle. Fear of one kind of Papist domination or another was given as the reason for the majority attitude but mutual hatred, fostered to a large extent by extremist clergy, also played its part. When 'normal' politics, the expected politics of a depressed industrial city, reared their salutary head it was usual and advantageous to play the Orange card.

As the low dishonest decade lurched towards its conclusion, it was clear that an economic upturn was likely and for the worst possible reasons. Another world war was to bring selective horror, this time to many more civilians, than in the Great War. For Belfast, except for the horrific spring of 1941, it was to have some positive aspects. The economy boomed; ships, both martial and commercial, had to be built. Linen and rope were to play their parts again in what became known, often ironically, as the 'war effort'. Belfast had begun a new industry sited on reclaimed land at Sydenham beside the new Belfast airport where Short Brothers of Rochester were subsidised by the government to combine with Harland & Wolff to build aeroplanes. The rate of unemployment eventually fell dramatically as planes and boats and tanks were produced. The number of Stirlings, the first of the heavy aircraft for use by Bomber Command that had been secretly designed and manufactured at Sydenham, came to a total of 2,381. The city manufactured 133 Sunderland flying-boats, 550 tanks (assembled at Carrickfergus), 170 smaller warships, and one aircraft carrier, the *Formidable*.

In spite of a reassuring speech by Craigavon, broadcast to the British people in 1939, in which he asserted: 'We are King's men and we shall be with you to the end,' not all Belfast people responded enthusiastically. The rump of the IRA reasserted its authority and started a bombing campaign in Britain but it was unsuccessful largely because de Valera interned suspects with much greater severity than Bates, allowing two hunger strikers to die. Some west Belfast activists were seen to burn the respirators supplied to every citizen and were accused hysterically of guiding the Luftwaffe during the air-raids.

There had been some enthusiastic enlistment in the first months of the war but it soon petered out. When, ignoring Churchill's advice, the government tried to impose conscription in 1941, it was vigorously opposed by the Nationalist population, led by Cardinal MacRory, but there was no great enthusiasm among Unionists either in spite of the government's offer. Memories of 25 years before had not been erased; besides, there were fears that the vacancies created would be filled by people from Éire. In Britain it was realised that conscription in the north might inhibit the large number of enlistments from the south. Between 1941 and 1945, 18,600 citizens of Éire joined up compared with 11,500 from the north.

The city, with full employment and many hours of overtime, was prosperous and after Pearl Harbor it was filled with US personnel as glamorous and exotic as if they had stepped down from the cinema screens. Belfast was no longer a staid provincial city but on six days of the week as colourful as Babylon or Vegas. The cinemas (and the children's playgrounds) stayed sabbatarianly closed. Labour relations were far from perfect. 320,000 working days were lost in the shipyard because of strikes, Short & Harland never managed more than 65 percent efficiency, and there were many stories of absenteeism and idleness. Stories like the following were so current as to have some basis in fact. A War Office official visiting the Sydenham plant asked a hand how many fighters he had made in the week. The workman replied, 'Oh; I suppose about twenty.' 'Twenty fighters in one week! Why that's magnificent! ' 'Fighters?' said the man. 'I thought you said *lighters*.' It was noticed too that hundreds of Belfast houses suddenly appeared painted in the dull shade of battleship grey.

The German occupation of northern France by the end of June 1940 and the setting up of a puppet state at Vichy brought the war closer to the city. As records were to show, the High Command had already obtained reconnaissance pictures of, among other installations, Shorts, Harland & Wolff, the Rank flourmills, the harbour power station and the waterworks. The vulnerability of the city to raids had been noted by John Clarke MacDermott (1896–1979), the Minister of Public Security, on 24 March 1941, as he advised John Millar Andrews (1871–1956), the new prime minister – Craigavon had died on 24 November 1940 – that the city had no fighter cover, no searchlights, no effective barrage balloons and less than half the recommended strength of anti-aircraft guns. He also said prophetically that he dreaded the next full moon.

Andrews had been an efficient Minister of Labour and of Finance but like many of his cabinet colleagues he was too old and too unimaginative to be a war leader. MacDermott was a more gifted official and afterwards became Lord Chief Justice. He had tried to get the Corporation to build air-raid shelters and recruit part-timers to the Auxiliary Fire Service (AFS) and the Air Raid Precautions service (ARP). The chief fire officer, with only 230 fire-fighters at his disposal, was incompetent and his immediate resignation had been recommended a month before the first blitz. There is anecdotal evidence that during the raids he hid under his desk weeping. His incompetence was typical of many inert Corporation officials, promoted without reference to ability.

The first visit from the Luftwaffe came on the night of 7–8 April 1941, the Monday and Tuesday of Holy Week. Bombs were falling even before the sirens were sounded. They killed 13 people, injured 81, flattened half of Harland & Wolff's yard, and extensively damaged the docks. It proved to be a taster for the following Easter Tuesday when, during a five-hour bombardment by a hundred planes, 200 tonnes of high explosive bombs, 76 drifting landmines and 29,000 incendiaries fell mainly on the crowded residential areas in the north city. It is thought that the raiders mistook the waterworks in that area for the Lagan and the result was a death toll of 900. Some Hurricane fighters were scrambled and what Ack-Ack guns that were serviceable pounded away. A single bomb hit the telephone exchange at the corner of Oxford Street and East Bridge Street, cutting off all communications with the artillery post, the Hurricanes' RAF base and Britain. Derry and Newtownards were also attacked that night but Belfast bore the brunt.

It was clear that there were no proper arrangements made for care of the homeless. The school and church halls, ill-prepared for the eventuality, could cope with no more than one tenth of the refugees and extreme measures were required to deal with the fatalities. The city mortuary could handle only 200 bodies so the Falls Road swimming baths were drained to take 150 more. The wide spaces of St George's Market housed about the same number and both locations attracted their quota of prurient and ghoulish voyeurs. Emma Duffin, a Belfastwoman who had been a nurse in the Great War, went to the market to offer professional assistance. She recorded in her diary the horror of what she saw:

> No attendant nurse had soothed the last moments of these victims, no gentle reverend hands had closed those eyes nor crossed those arms. With tangled, staring eyes, clutching hands, contorted limbs, their grey green faces covered with dust they lay bundled into the coffins, half shrouded in rugs or blankets or an occasional sheet, still wearing their dirty torn twisted garments.

The blitz, as these things often do, brought out the best and worst in the people of Belfast. The nightly excursions to the safety of the hills and glens of up to 10,000 people made strangers into acquaintances. Fortunately the weather was mild. Many people from the Protestant Shankill fleeing further night raids found themselves fellow refugees with Catholics from the Falls when they secured shelter in the deep cellars of Clonard Monastery, sited strategically between the two usually inimical areas. Extremists on both sides were not convinced. The non-significant fact that many Catholic areas suffered little and no Catholic churches were damaged while many Protestant churches were destroyed brought the old atavistic suspicions to the surface again. Nationalists had guided the German planes with torches, some insisted, and someone with an enviable sense of the surreal suggested that the 'Pope was in the first aeroplane'. (The thought of the austere 65-year-old Pius XII in a flying-suit sitting up in the nose of a Heinkel is more than bizarre.) One of the reasons for the greater destruction of Protestant churches was that there were many more of them in the sabbatarian city and the concentration of bombs in Protestant districts was caused by their proximity to the intended targets.

Stories abounded: a Protestant shop in York Street that had, it was said, displayed a carcase with a notice saying, 'This pig was cured at Lourdes,' was believed to have received a direct hit. Extremists were not sure how to react to the fact that de Valera sent 13 fire appliances and 65 fire-fighters from Dun Laoghaire, Dublin, Drogheda and Dundalk. They found their way in the blackout by following the telegraph poles. Alfie Byrne (1882–1956), Dublin's colourful lord mayor, was believed to have travelled in one of the engines to show urban solidarity.

Two hundred bombers returned on 4 May on the kind of bright moonlit night that MacDermott had dreaded. They inflicted great damage on Shorts, the shipyard, where three corvettes ready for launching were destroyed, York Street station and the power station. There were fewer civilian casualties because their tactical targets were laid out as on an illuminated map for them and because the 'ditchers', as the nocturnal refugees were called, still used the country as a refuge. One hundred and fifty people died and 157 were seriously injured. Those ditchers watching from Cave Hill could see nothing but a city turned into an inferno. The fire service's hoses went dry because water mains had been ruptured in the bombardment and the tidal Lagan could not be reached by the pumps.

Those catastrophic nights in May were not repeated, the city saved by Hitler's decision to march on Moscow. Still the ditchers trooped out of the crowded streets and evacuation of children, which had collapsed at first trial due to a mixture of incompetence and the evacuees' unofficial return home, was reintroduced. The condition of the children – undersized, unhealthy, lice-infested, and in the words of Bates, 'unbilletable' – produced condemnation from the unfortunate people on whom they were billeted and the geriatric cabinet, whose greater concern was the protection of LS Merrifield's (1880–1943) statue of Carson that menaced the long avenue up to the parliament buildings at Stormont. They could not see that the condemnation was more fitly directed at them and the Corporation. At least the latter paid the price for incompetence, corruption and sheer lack of commonsense. The government replaced it by a three-man commission led by a civil servant, CW Grant, in June 1942 that had for a period of three and a half years the powers relinquished by the Corporation. The prime minister was ousted by cabinet colleagues led by the equally hardline but slightly more dynamic Sir Basil Brooke on 30 April 1943.

For the rest of the war Belfast prospered. There was virtually full employment in a city that bulged with allied forces, especially Americans who were lavish in their generosity to Belfast children with Hershey and Baby Ruth candy bars and unfiltered carcinogenic Camel, Lucky Strike and Philip Morris cigarettes for their parents. Belfast people came to realise what being a citizen of a really rich country meant and they were geared to demand more after hostilities ceased. Under the lend-lease system agreed by Churchill and President Roosevelt, as well as battle ships and armaments, British children were given free cod-liver oil and concentrated orange juice. The dancehalls flourished, with those unique Belfast institutions, the dance studios, holding their own against the larger venues, though none had the elegance of the art-deco Floral Hall built in Hazelwood and offering romantic views of the lough. The cinemas in their full glory never lacked a queue for the 'second house' and one, the Broadway on the Falls Road, was used by the Derry IRA volunteer Hugh McAteer and his colleague Jimmy Steele as a venue for an Easter Commemoration of 'those who had died for Ireland' on Holy Saturday 1943. They had escaped from Crumlin Road gaol in January and were subsequently rearrested. Their flamboyant gesture was little more than a piece of agitprop for the IRA that was all but moribund in the city.

Legitimate drama had at least a silver age during the war partly because of the Ulster Group Theatre (1941–1960) that, unlike the ULT, had a permanent home in the Ulster Minor Hall. The actors were originally amateur but they soon became professional under the guidance of directors Harold Goldblatt, with a later career in films, and James Mageean. Such well-known names as Joseph Tomelty, JG Devlin, Margaret D'Arcy, James Ellis, Patrick Magee, Stephen Boyd, Allan McClelland, Elizabeth Begley and Denys Hawthorne began their careers with the Group. In the war years the company could count on full houses and, with the repertory company of the Savoy Players in the Opera House, brightened the gloom of winter blackouts. Plays were written by the old ULT hand George Shiels, with new tailormade dramas by Jack Loudan, Patricia O'Connor and Tomelty.

The misery of rationing, especially of tea, butter, sugar, tinned goods, biscuits, sweets and meat was mitigated somewhat by the availability of liquor, sugar, butter and meat in Éire. Efficient personal smuggling, a two-way system, taking tea to Dundalk and bringing their goods to Newry, eased the hardship for those who could afford to use the system. Those without the means had to suffer some form of rationing until it finally ceased in 1955.

Literature prospered in an unassuming Belfast way. The unselfconscious coterie who gathered in Campbell's Coffee House in Donegall Square West were described by Sam Hanna Bell, one of their number, as 'young men with a terrible thirst for culture'. They included John Boyd (1912–2001), later talks producer with BBC NI, Denis Ireland (1894–1974), William Conor, Joe Tomelty (1911–95) and 'Richard Rowley' – Richard Valentine Williams (1877–1947). Irregulars were John Hewitt (1907–87), Lynn Doyle, Rutherford Mayne and Cathal O'Shannon (1889–1969), the socialist. One day in 1943 Rowley announced that he was funding a publishing house, Mourne Press, and that among the first titles would be the short story collections, *The White Mare* by Michael McLaverty, already an established writer, and *Summer Loanen* by Bell. The instincts of these young men replicated that of Hobson and Parkhill when they damned Yeats. Since 1941 *The Bell,* a brilliant literary journal printed on the cheapest of paper and edited by Sean O'Faolain, had shaken neutral Éire to its isolationist core. Now Bell and Boyd produced four editions of a Belfast equivalent, with the equally non-commital title *Lagan.* The first wary edition came out in 1943 and continued until 1946, publishing material by Tomelty, McLaverty, WR Rodgers (1909–

69), Maurice James Craig (b. 1919), Robert Greacen (1920–2008), Roy McFadden (1921–99) and the two founders. It was a remarkable publication to have had its birth in wartime Belfast and served as a reminder that there was more to the city than industry and sectarianism.

All in all, the 1941 bombardments aside, as fortunate ex-servicemen were said to remark, 'They hadn't such a bad war.'

12

Peace and Prosperity

BELFAST SOON RECOVERED FROM THE WAR but the people faced nearly ten years of further austerity. The arctic winter of 1947 is still part of the city's folklore but it was followed by a glorious summer. Coal when it could be mined could not be transported and all feared not only that there would be few spring flowers but no non-migratory birds would have survived the fierce winter cold. Their fears were groundless; there were bright sunshiny days right from Easter till October.

There was a lot to talk about and since it was the beginning of a long period of urban peace some of the conversations were with separated brethren. The Labour landslide in the post-war election enabled Clement Attlee (1883–1967) to pass the most complete package of welfare legislation since that of the Liberals in 1906. The National Health Service (NHS) gave free medical care from birth to death and after. People, who could not have afforded them before, got free prescription drugs, dentures and spectacles, and families got an allowance for each child after the first. This original payment of 25 pence per child was gradually increased and paid for all the children, the money going directly to the mother, and later called Child Benefit.

Yet even here sectarian politics eventually obtruded. In 1956 Ivan Neill, the Minister of Finance, brought in a bill that proposed that the family allowance should not be paid to the younger children of larger families. The reasons given were fiscal probity and good husbandry, and there was no suggestion that its main impetus was against Catholics. They were, however, believed with some statistical evidence to be the main beneficiaries of the system. Even if this were absolutely true they needed state aid more than those with fewer children. Catholics immediately protested and two bishops from the dioceses of Derry and Dromore travelled to make their protest in person. Sir Basil Brooke (Viscount Brookeborough since 1952) was summoned to Westminster in June and returned to announce that Northern Ireland would continue to keep pace with Britain.

Another problem with the health service was not so easily solved. The Mater Infirmorum, the sole Catholic hospital in Northern Ireland, sited incidentally in a largely Protestant district at the foot of the Crumlin Road, was not able for reasons of canon law to surrender itself to state control. Equivalent institutions in Britain were allowed to claim for the expenses of the A&E services that they provided free without regard to class or creed but this was not permitted to the Mater. Again voluntary funding was provided by an ad hoc group calling itself the Young Philanthropists that ran the YP pools to supplement the hospital's finances. It was not until 1971 that the Mater, its ethos maintained, was able to avail itself of the government grants.

The 1947 Education Act that replicated the act of 1944 sponsored by RA Butler (1902–82) gave free appropriate second and third-level education to those judged capable of receiving it. Previous to this bill the state did little more than insist on attendance at public elementary school. True 'necessitous children' were provided with free books and free meals, with voluntary bodies like Toc H and SVP subsidising the scheme. Only 50 scholarships, 30 for boys and 20 for girls, were provided by the Corporation for attendances at city grammar schools. Some schools had foundation scholarships and the city's assistance for university attendance, five scholarships worth £160, had continued at that low level since 1913. The necessary negotiations were complicated by the appointment by Brookeborough of Harry Midgley (1892–1957), a man whose anti-Catholicism was public knowledge, as Minister of Education in 1950. He had once been a socialist and a vocal supporter of the government side in the Spanish Civil War (1936–9). In several public debates his version of events in Catalonia was challenged by a Catholic priest, Dr Arthur H Ryan (1897–1972), then lecturer in Scholastic Philosophy at Queen's University Belfast, and believing he had been publicly humiliated, Midgley became even more anti-clerical. He joined the Unionist Party in 1947 and was duly rewarded.

Dr Mageean, like other bishops in Northern Ireland, could not allow education to become state controlled and so was faced by a colossal financial burden to provide the new schools. The bishops further felt that Protestants, having been granted the right to have the Protestant ethos maintained in the 'state' schools, were given full grants while Catholics had had to make do with 60 percent grants. Lt-Col Samuel Hall-Thompson (1885–1954), the previous minister, had increased this grant from 50 percent and proposed to pay Catholic teachers' national insurance and superannuation. When he heard that Brookeborough had attended a meeting to object to this, he had no alternative but to resign. Midgley's appointment was clearly to prevent any such favouring of Catholics but his permanent officials, who regarded his appointment as mischievous, were able to save much of Hall-Thompson's original bill. By 1968 the Catholic clergy were sufficiently confident of the government's good intentions that they subscribed to the 'Four and Two' Committee system that allowed them the same grants as state schools. The 'Eleven-Plus' selection examination made grammar school education available to all who might benefit from it. It resulted in a kind of social revolution that would affect Northern Ireland in future decades.

The city bloomed in the post-war atmosphere that saw the lowest level of sectarian tension since the state's foundation. Churchill's 'dreary steeples' did not disappear but relief, exhaustion and a sense that the city had been spared the worst of the horrors made commonsense prevail.

BBC NI entered a kind of golden age largely due to the work of Sam Hanna Bell and John Boyd. There was often input, too, from JJ Campbell (1910–79) who was afterwards Director of the Institute of Education at Queen's, causing one wit to suggest that the marvellous radio output from Ormeau Avenue in the 1950s was a magical mixture of Bell, Boyd and Campbell. The service had begun on 15 September 1924 from a studio in 31 Linenhall Street as 2BE, the Belfast Station of the British Broadcasting Corporation, as its first announcer, the young Tyrone Guthrie (1900–71), described it, and successive controllers made its output safe for Unionism. One early director, George L Marshall, objected to a programme to be called *The Irish* in 1937, stating: 'There is no such thing today as an Irishman. One is either a citizen of the Irish Free State or a citizen of the United Kingdom of Great Britain and Northern Ireland.'

Things changed after Bell was appointed by Louis MacNeice, then of the famous London Features Department, as Features Producer answerable to Portland Place and not to the right-wing establishment in Ormeau Avenue. He produced many programmes about Ulster life and history, many written by himself and others by WR Rodgers, Roy McFadden and Sam Thompson (1916–65), who later wrote the explosive *Over the Bridge* (1957). Campbell wrote six memorable features, including *Dove Over the Water* (1954), about St Colum Cille, and *Wee Joe* (1959), about Belfast's favourite politician. With Sean O'Boyle (1908–79) and Michael J Murphy (1913–96), Bell assembled a rich archive of Ulster song and folklore. John Boyd's programmes, notably *Your Questions,* to which JJ Campbell was a frequent contributor, dared to air topics such as religion, politics and sectarianism hitherto embargoed.

Bell's four novels *December Bride* (1951), *The Hollow Ball* (1965), *A Man Flourishing* (1973) and *Across the Narrow Sea* (1987), though essentially historical, give great insight into the nature of his city. His friend Michael McLaverty, too, wrote many novels and even finer short stories about city life. Younger novelists, Brian Moore (1921–99) and Maurice Leitch (b. 1933) faced the contradictions of Belfast life with great verve and courage, forcing it into the world's consciousness, a process continued by Glenn Patterson (b. 1961) and Robert McLiam Wilson (b. 1964).

Poets continued to portray the city, a task begun by MacNeice and furthered by John Hewitt, Roy McFadden and Robert Greacen. By the early 1960s a charismatic mentor, Philip Hobsbaum (1932–2005), had gathered round him in Queen's a singing school of younger poets, Seamus Heaney (b. 1939), later winner of the Nobel Prize for literature, Michael Longley (b. 1939) and Derek Mahon (b. 1941). Each was to deal in personal idiosyncratic ways with the Ulster troubles while arrogating to themselves the right to choose other topics.

Belfast, as its industrial days slipped away and shipbuilding, linen and ropeworks no longer dominated world markets, recovered something of its old eighteenth-century reputation as a place of culture. Yet the hyena of sectarianism was not dead but merely slept. Sam Thompson's play *Over the Bridge*, about religious hatred and violence in the shipyard, accepted by the Group in 1957, was withdrawn when the management lost its nerve because of the play's theme. Thompson had learned his trade – as a writer, that is; he was a painter in Harland & Wolff before this – devising such features as *Brush in Hand* (1954) and *General Foreman* (1956) for Sam Hanna Bell. James Ellis (b. 1931) resigned as artistic director and the Group seemed to disintegrate. Ellis directed the play with great success in the old Empire Theatre in January 1960.

Other theatre ventures included the Belfast Arts Theatre, begun by Dorothy and Hubert Wilmot in the 1940s, and after several addresses, including Linenhall Street, Upper North Street, Fountain Street Mews and Little Donegall Street, found a suitable home in a purpose-built theatre in Botanic Avenue where actors and audiences had regularly to contend with the noise of trains rattling through the tunnel beneath. It proved to be an early victim of the Troubles, closing in 1971, though the theatre is still used. The Wilmots' ideal was to provide Belfast with the best of international drama, much as the Gate Theatre in Dublin was intended to provide. The Lyric Players Theatre, the poetic child of Mary (1918–2006) and Pearse O'Malley (d. 2004), was set up in 1951 in Pearse's consulting room, an annex of their home in Derryvolgie Avenue. It originated in Mary O'Malley's passion for the plays of Yeats – hence the gibe: 'Hail Mary full of Yeats' – and in the little domestic theatre and later in the Lyric, built in Ridgeway Street, off the Stranmillis Road, all of his plays were done. The theatre remains as the O'Malleys' legacy.

As the 1950s became the 1960s a new generation of what could be called Beveridge children grew up.[1] There was less need for emigration among working-class Catholics, who always valued education as the one source of advancement. Life was easier but they were still cut off from preferment in the public sector of employment and much of the private.

The city was also changing. Shipbuilding orders had become scarce, though the launch of the *Canberra*, the last great passenger ship built by Harland & Wolff, in 1960, showed that the Island could still deliver the goods, and Admiralty orders for three aircraft carriers, *Eagle*, *Centaur* and *Bulwark*, had kept the company afloat during the 1950s. The *Canberra* for all its opulence had been built at a loss and the company continued to lose money, while ironically improving the techniques that allowed it to build oilrigs and tankers. The giant crane Goliath joined Samson to become the city's identifiable landmarks, just as Big Ben in the clock tower of St Stephen identifies London, but there was less need for them. Orders continued to diminish; the company, debilitated by management conservatism, was privatised in 1989 when it employed less than 3,000 workers; in

1914 it had employed 14,000. Now it is used mainly for ship repairs and is in the process of becoming a heritage area.

The rest of the industries that made the city's reputation – linen, rope, engineering, tobacco – showed the same slow decline. By the millennium a lot of employment was in the public sector.

Sectarian strife in Belfast in the two decades after the war had been low key, weathering the shock announcement by John A[loysius] Costello (1891–1976), the Taoiseach of the Irish coalition government, at a press conference on 7 September 1948 in Ottawa, of his intention to remove Éire from the Commonwealth and declare it a republic. Brookeborough and his Unionist cabinet were quickly in touch with Attlee who reassured them on 3 May 1949 that Northern Ireland would continue to be part of the Commonwealth and made it binding with the Ireland Act on 2 June. Belfast Nationalists were disappointed but not surprised and bore this latest blow with their usual non-violent stoicism. The Border Campaign of the resurgent IRA (1956–62) had little impact and less support in the city. The immediate internment by Brian Faulkner (1921–77), Minister of Home Affairs – that rarity at the time, a Unionist member of cabinet who was young and talented – of known IRA members, and a similar initiative by de Valera in the republic, effectively defeated Operation Harvest, as it was called.

Brookeborough resigned on 25 March 1963 and was replaced by Terence O'Neill, who was sufficiently aware of the growing impatience of Nationalists about their inferior status as citizens and realised the need for some kind of reform. Yet when a monolith makes an attempt at self-reformation it makes current politics very volatile.

Protestant grassroots had noticed a new confidence among young Catholic graduates, products of the Education Act, who were no longer content to accept the 50-year-old acquiescence in the partial state of Northern Ireland. The exuberance of the 1960s with such essentially revolutionary events as the Second Vatican Council (1962–5), the growth of the youth cult and the total dissemination of television was bound to change society. Fundamental Protestantism was inclined to resist the new spirit of the age and it found its champion in the charismatic Rev Ian Paisley (b. 1926), a man of great physical strength and stentorian voice, who seemed like a reincarnation of 'Roaring' Hanna with a confident stand-up comedian's command of audience. Paisley seemed to target O'Neill like a heat-seeking missile, finally defeating him in his hitherto safe Bannside seat in 1970.

Paisley had already made a name for himself with various incidents in the 1950s and 1960s. He had organised a march to the City Hall to protest about the Corporation's decision to fly the flag at half-mast to honour the death of Pope John XXIII (1881–1963).[2] In 1958 he had accused the Queen Mother and Princess Margaret, the queen's sister, of 'spiritual fornication and adultery with the Anti-Christ' because they had visited the pope. His interference in the 1964 imperial election led to two days of old-style riots in Divis Street at the foot of the Falls Road and, when O'Neill precipitately invited the Irish Taoiseach, Sean Lemass (1899–1971), to Stormont for trade talks in 1965, and Lemass, with even greater courage, accepted, since the visit gave de facto recognition to the Northern Ireland state, Paisley led a vociferous opposition to the apparent détente. 'O'Neill must go!', his banner campaign, was eventually successful because he went and by that time city and country were in turmoil. Nationalists were initially pleased with O'Neill's rather vague liberal pronouncements but it was clear that most of his cabinet did not share his views, especially Faulkner.

The fiftieth anniversaries of both the Easter Rising and the Battle of the Somme were celebrated in 1966, increasing tension. Unionist headquarters in Glengall Street was fire-bombed, as was a Catholic primary school on the Crumlin Road. Paisley led a loyalist march through the Catholic Markets area and was sent to jail for three months, having refused to keep the peace after creating a disturbance outside the Presbyterian General Assembly. More ominous was the rise of a Protestant paramilitary force calling itself the UVF, after

Carson's volunteer force, that shot three Catholics in Malvern Street, off the Shankill Road, on 26 June, one of whom died of his wounds.

In February 1967 a number of reformist groups banded together to form the Northern Ireland Civil Rights Association to begin a campaign, modelled on Martin Luther King's crusade in America. It held several marches for freedom, culminating in a banned march in Derry on 5 October 1968, which was televised and showed how marchers, including a number of MPs – Eddie McAteer (1914–86), head of the Nationalist Party, Gerry Fitt (1926–2005), Republican Labour, and three Labour backbenchers who had come straight from the Party Conference – and bystanders alike were attacked by baton, boot and water cannon by the RUC.

Northern Ireland's guilty secret was out: this was how legitimate protest was dealt with there. Until 1969 Belfast was only minimally involved in the riots, violence and marches that afflicted mainly the west of the province. O'Neill rushed through a reform package, inevitably greeted with the cry, 'Too little – too late.' He was brought down by a cabinet revolt hastened by a UVF bombing campaign that included an attack on the Silent Valley reservoir, Belfast's main source of water, and electricity sub-stations.[3] His replacement, almost a doppelgänger, James Chichester-Clarke (1923–2002), tried to prevent chaos. Tension increased during the summer marching season, breaking into riot especially around the Nationalist Unity Flats complex at the foot of the Protestant Shankill, but it was the Apprentice Boys march in Derry on 12 August and the Battle of the Bogside that followed that started the conflagration that lasted for more than 35 years.

The battle raged for three days with liberal use of CS gas by the RUC and much throwing of rocks and petrol bombs from the beleaguered inhabitants of the Bogside with help from other parts of the Nationalist city. A forgivable but injudicious call for sympathetic action in other Nationalist parts of the North was made by such defenders as Bernadette Devlin (b. 1947). She was the youngest woman MP and had run the gauntlet of the Protestant attack on the People's Democracy march at Burntollet Bridge on 4 January 1969. Such support was not in fact needed because the battle finished by 5pm on 14 August when, to general jubilation, soldiers of the Queen's Own were deployed in Derry streets.

That night Protestants, perhaps interpreting the Bogsiders' call for help as a call for a general uprising – though, considering the numbers of opposing sides, hardly a real fear – supported by the well-armed UVF, invaded the Catholic districts of the Lower Falls and Ardoyne, killing five Catholics, and destroying nearly 200 Catholic homes. The priests of the Passionist Order who ministered to the parish of Ardoyne, dreading another night of Protestant violence, begged James Callaghan (1912–2005), the Home Secretary, to authorise peace-keeping troops in Belfast, as well as in Derry. The British army had arrived but no one could have foreseen how long it would be before they could leave.

Things went quiet and there was great rejoicing in the Nationalist community. Protestants felt betrayed; their usual allies, the British government, had turned against them and the Fenians (to some Protestants, the hated Fenians) had won some kind of unspecific advantage. On the night of 11–12 October, a crowd, aware that the B-Specials were about to be disbanded, advanced menacingly towards Unity Flats. The army was called in and the first casualty of the renewed violence was an RUC constable, Victor Arbuckle. Two civilians also died in fire between the army and the UVF.

It seemed that the army was on the side of Nationalists but this was to change with the resurgence of the IRA. They had been pilloried in August because of their inadequacy in protecting Catholics; graffiti reading 'IRA: I ran away' rankled but, as ever, 'England's difficulty was Ireland's opportunity.' They reformed and made the 'Brits', the RUC, and the Ulster Defence Regiment (UDR) – the USC's replacement, and essentially defeating the purpose of the change by having largely the same personnel – their main military targets. An internal split produced two bodies: those who wished to take part in such constitutional activities as fighting elections and were known from 11 January 1970 as the Official IRA (OIRA) and an obstinately abstentionist group calling themselves the Provisional IRA (PIRA), known thereafter as the 'Provos'. Both targeted the security forces but owing to public revulsion at the Aldershot bomb (February 1972), which killed five civilians, and the callous killing of trooper William Best, a young Derry soldier home on leave, on 20 May 1972, the 'Stickies', as the OIRA were called, declared a ceasefire on 29 May. The Provos, however, with an almost religious devotion to the 'armed struggle' that was in their eyes the only means of achieving a united and independent Ireland, continued their campaign of bombing economic targets and killing any of the different security forces.

The first military victim of the PIRA campaign was Gunner Robert Curtis who was shot during rioting in the New Lodge Road on 6 February 1971. A month later, on 10 March, three off-duty Scottish soldiers were lured to their deaths by IRA women volunteers. On 18 August 1969 Lieutenant-General Sir Ian Freeland, GOC of the British army, commenting upon the ecstatic welcome given to the soldiers in Derry and Belfast said, 'Honeymoons can be very short-lived.' It was certainly over in Belfast. The first indication that the soldiers might no longer be the friend of Nationalists was the illegal 36-hour curfew begun on 3 July 1970 as the army with considerable violence searched 5,000 homes in the Lower Falls, leaving the people with no means of obtaining food for their children. They found some arms but, as the victims observed, they would have had much richer pickings if they had carried out the same operation in the Shankill. Six civilians died in the rioting that followed. It was believed that it was by the direct order of the new Conservative prime minister, Edward Heath (1916–2005), that the incursion was made and that he had insisted that Bernadette Devlin should be tried for her part in the Battle of the Bogside.

There had been a change of prime minister in Northern Ireland as well. Brian Faulkner had succeeded Chichester-Clarke, who was more than happy to go, in March 1971. Faulkner was more acceptable to extreme Unionism; he was known to have helped undermine O'Neill authority. He was also convinced that he could again defeat the IRA as he had done in Operation Harvest.

On 9 August 1971, under pressure from, among others, the shipyard workers, and with extremely reluctant agreement from Westminster, he announced internment. It was a brilliant recruiting drive for the IRA and hardened attitudes even among moderate Nationalists. Almost all of the 343 arrested (and treated to all the illegal methods of modern interrogation) were Catholic and none were significant members of the IRA; the Special Branch's list was woefully out of date. In the riots that followed eleven civilians and one soldier died, including Fr Hugh Murray, who was shot while administering the last rites in Ballymurphy. Apart from engendering a total lack of confidence in the impartiality of the law in Northern Ireland internment led indirectly to one of the most horrific of all the events of those latest Troubles. It was during an anti-internment march on 30 January 1972 that 13 innocent marchers were killed by paratroopers, on what seemed to be deliberately punitive incursion.[4] Many uncommitted young people of both sexes rushed to join the PIRA and the stage was set for bloody attrition.

The immediate and dramatic effect of the carnage on Bloody Sunday, as the grisly event has since been called, was the abolition of the Stormont parliament by Heath on 24 March 1972. It had lasted 50 years and 291 days since it first met on 7 June 1921 in the City Hall. Now Northern Ireland would be subject to the direct rule of a secretary of state from the Northern Ireland Office (NIO).

Northern Ireland was to have Secretaries of State, eight from the Labour Party: Merlyn Rees (1974–6), Roy Mason (September 1976–9), Mo Mowlam (1997–9), Peter Mandelson (1999–2001), John Reid (2001–2), Paul Murphy (2002–5), Peter Hain (2005–7) – he also served as secretary for Wales – and Shaun Woodward (2007–

10); and nine Conservatives: William Whitelaw (1972–3), Francis Pym (1973–4), Humphrey Atkins (1979–81), James Prior (1981–4), Douglas Hurd (1984–5), Tom King (1985–9), Sir Peter Brooke (1989–92), Sir Patrick Mayhew (1992–7) and Owen Patterson (2010–). They varied in personality and in achievement. Whitelaw proved nearly the most successful, bringing the North to accept a power-sharing executive with the Sunningdale Conference in December 1973. His replacement after a general election by Pym did not halt the process but eleven out of twelve seats were won by anti-Sunningdale candidates.

The power-sharing body, with Brian Faulkner as chief executive and Gerry Fitt of the recently formed Social Democratic and Labour Party (SDLP) as second minister, began its brief existence on 1 January 1974. John Hume, another founder of the SDLP, became Minister of Finance. It lasted until 28 May when Faulkner resigned and the executive was again replaced by direct rule after the successful and frightening Ulster Workers Council (UWC) strike, supported by the Ulster Defence Association (UDA), a new Protestant paramilitary organisation founded at the time of internment. Rees, who had become Secretary of State in March, underestimated the intensity of feelings of the Protestant people, especially in the city. It was felt that he could have insisted that the army could at least man the petrol-pumps. It also seemed incredible that in the whole of the army there could not be found enough engineers to provide some power. The trump card of the UWC was this support of the power workers. Electricity cuts were widespread and though the army *had* taken over some of the filling stations for their own needs there was no petrol available for ordinary people. Roadblocks sealed off the inner city and members of the UDA were seen to fraternise with RUC officers who did nothing to keep the highways open. What caused the greatest anxiety was that the reduction of electric generation to ten percent and the removal of key workers, demanded by the UWC, would cause the sewers to back up.

13

War and Peace

THERE WAS GENERAL JUBILATION IN PROTESTANT areas at the fall of the executive and the fact that no deaths were reported in the city was something of a relief.[1] Belfast's bloodiest year had been 1972: on 4 March two people had died and 136 were injured in an IRA bomb in the Abercorn Restaurant in Castle Place; on 28 May an IRA bomb, exploding prematurely, killed eight people in Short Strand; but the most serious incident occurred on 21 July 1972 when a total of eleven people, including women and children, were killed in a series of IRA explosions, 22 in all, in the city centre.

Just before the start of the UWC strike there had been a UVF attack on 2 May in the Rose and Crown pub in the Ormeau Road, when five people were killed and 17 injured. The city was to experience similar atrocities during the next 20 years. On 5 April 1975 four civilians and one serving member of the UDR were killed in an IRA bomb attack in the Mountainview Tavern on the Shankill, and one week later, probably in retaliation, six people died when the Strand Bar, Short Strand was bombed by the UVF. The IRA bombed the Baynardo Bar in the Shankill on 13 August the same year, a reprisal it was believed for the murderous attack by the UVF on the Miami Showband less than a fortnight before.

Violence was distributed unfairly throughout Northern Ireland

and Belfast, considering its size and population density, did not fare as ill as might have been expected. Individual horrors like the IRA fire-bombing of the Le Mon restaurant on 17 February 1978, when twelve guests at a dinner died, stayed longer in the public memory than such 'run-of-the-mill' affairs as the UVF's attack on the Chlorane Bar in Gresham Street, with five casualties, on 5 June 1976, or the UFF's shooting of five punters in Sean Graham's betting shop on the Ormeau Road on 5 February 1992. The last grisly spectacular the city suffered was the explosion on 23 October 1993 above a fish shop in the Lower Shankill when nine shoppers died as well as one of the IRA bombers.

There were other dark events associated with the deepening civil war. The 1981 hunger strike by IRA and INLA prisoners for political status in the Maze prison (1 March–3 October), during which ten prisoners died, increased tension excruciatingly throughout the North.[2] The death toll due to violent incidents during the protest was 64.

The Troubles darkened life throughout Northern Ireland and Belfast shared in the stygian gloom. Yet life persisted, as it instinctively does. A generation grew up that had never experienced peace. They had never known the city when it was free from the threat of shooting and bombing; they accepted the travel restrictions, the permanent checkpoints that protected town centres and the temporary ones that could be imposed by the simple juxtaposition of two Land Rovers, as well as the luggage and body searches before entry to shop, bank or post office. Though there were 'spectaculars', as notable paramilitary shootings or bombings came to be called, the 'long war' never again had the same intensity as in the earlier years. The death total due to the security situation for 1972 was 470 and by the next year it had dropped to 252. Of 3,289 deaths, the total for the years 1969–98, the years 1990–98 accounted for only 502.

Succeeding secretaries of state tried to find a working devolution and peace. The first move came surprisingly during the premiership of Margaret Thatcher (b. 1925) who had proved very much the 'iron lady' of her publicity. The Anglo-Irish Agreement (AIA) of 1985 did something to suggest a way forward. It established the right of the people of Northern Ireland to determine its own future and provided a significant role for the Dublin government.

Belfast people did their best to keep cheerful as one act of violence followed another, and tried to live ordinary lives. They did this with the assumption that the Troubles, as they understated the situation, might not affect them. They kept the same sane detachment from the writhings and gyrations of what was later known as the 'peace process'. The swan of peace had indeed begun to make her stately glide across the troubled waters but the ferocious working of her legs beneath the surface that made progress possible was the endlessly patient work of such people as Thatcher's successor John Major (b. 1943), Albert Reynolds (b. 1932) when Taoiseach, John Hume and Gerry Adams (b. 1948), who proved the leading statesman of Sinn Féin, an old name resurrected to describe the IRA's political manifestation.

The AIA was welcomed enthusiastically by Nationalists and rejected by Unionists. A banner across the classical pediment of the City Hall reading 'Ulster Says No!' stayed in place for several years. One Christmas it was altered with unusual wit to 'Ulster Says Noel.' The progress made by the AIA was furthered on 15 December 1993 by the significant Downing Street Declaration by Major and Reynolds. It was an ambiguously worded document and without alienating the Unionists gave Sinn Féin a role. It had too the approval of the immensely powerful and brilliantly persuasive United States President Bill Clinton (b. 1946).

Belfast shuddered with the shocks of the bad news and flourished in the gradually easing of tensions over the next 14 or so years. The IRA ceasefire of August 1994 was relished by most of its citizens and after the loyalist ceasefire in October the city began to blossom with a relaxed nightlife unknown for decades. That nightlife staggered a little when the IRA bomb at Canary Wharf on 9 February 1996 ended their cessation but it recovered when the new secretary of state Mo Mowlam helped smooth away many of the besetting political difficulties. The Belfast Agreement, signed on Good Friday, 10 April 1998, a day after the deadline set by Clinton's chairman, the cheerful and preternaturally patient Senator George Mitchell (b. 1933), caused a great surge of hope. Clinton promised $100 million dollars in economic aid, and a legislative assembly that included Sinn Féin ministers was elected in November 1999. It was suspended in February 2000 and restored in May the same year. The problem was an apparent reluctance on the part of the IRA to prove decommissioning of arms and explosives. Except for the exasperating lack of resolution it could have been seen as a highly entertaining if too long-running soap opera. David Trimble (b. 1944), who had become head of the Unionist Party in September 1995, resigned on 7 May 2005, having lost his Upper Bann seat in the British general election and 13 months later became Baron Trimble of Lisnagarvey. He later joined the Conservatives, sitting with that party in the House of Lords.

That election made it clear that the two leading political parties in Northern Ireland had become Sinn Féin and the Democratic Unionist Party (DUP). Ian Paisley had founded the party as a means of expressing the true views of grassroots Unionism in 1971. The result marginalised the slightly more centrist SDLP and Ulster Unionist Party (UUP), the rump of the party that had ruled Northern Ireland since 1921.

The problem of IRA decommissioning proved gradually soluble. Another breakthrough came with the wary acceptance of the St Andrews Agreement by the DUP in October 2006 and many with fingers crossed awaited the outcome of fresh assembly elections set for 7 March. Sinn Féin's acceptance of the Police Service of Northern Ireland (PSNI) – the new force proposed by Chris Patten (b. 1944) in his eponymous report – eased Unionist suspicions. They deeply regretted the standing down of the RUC in November 2001 but were reassured by the personality and performance of Sir Hugh Orde (b. 1958), the second chief constable. Nationalists agreed but were more enthusiastic about Nuala O'Loan (b. 1951), the Police Ombundsman, than some Unionists.

Not unexpectedly the DUP became the largest party in the assembly with 36 seats; Sinn Féin caused no surprise by coming second with 28; the UUP under Trimble's replacement, Sir Reg Empey (b. 1947), came third with 18 seats, and the SDLP, under its vigorous young leader Mark Durkan (b. 1960), was fourth with 16. The new assembly met for the first time on 8 May 2007 and there seemed from the start to be more than just accommodation between Ian Paisley and Sinn Féin's Martin McGuinness as first and second ministers of Northern Ireland's devolved administration.

The way ahead is full of all kinds of possibilities, both daunting and challenging, but there is in the province and in the city a more than cautious optimism. The last 40 years or so have tested Belfast to the limit but she still survives as a worthy and fascinating city, perhaps with a more hopeful future than her bloody but unbowed citizens ever thought to hope for. The Macrory Report implemented in 1972 reduced the Corporation to the level of a district council. It hurt the feelings of the city fathers who had always regarded the Stormont government as 'Johnnies-come-lately' to have their powers reduced, as someone bitterly described it, to 'bins, bogs and burials'.

Even after the intermittent peace process had calmed the city there were still shocks felt within the conurbation from events elsewhere. The recurring annual stand-off at Drumcree Church in Portadown by Orangemen wanting to walk down the Garvaghy Road, their traditional route, and being prevented from doing so by police and army first gave trouble in 1996. The old return route was no longer a country lane but the main road through a Nationalist estate. Trouble was at its greatest in 1997 when Orangemen throughout the North disrupted travel, blocked roads and bridges, tossed breezeblocks on to the M2 motorway and hijacked cars on the approach to the city.

In recent years the Garvaghy Road has become a relatively quiet part of the colourful tapestry that is the Ulster summer.

Belfast had another spasm of publicity as a sectarian city with the Holy Cross incident in September 2001. Catholic schoolgirls, including first-timers, were forced to run the gauntlet of loyalist attack as they made their way to school at Ardoyne past the Protestant Glenbryn estate. Bricks, bags of urine and worse, even a bomb, were thrown as the terrified children were hustled past on their way to Holy Cross Girls Primary School on the other side of the Ardoyne Road. Sectarian tension had been characteristic of the summer. Nothing else can explain the noisy viciousness of the protesters, especially the women. The sectarian deaths of four Protestants and two Catholics in that early autumn were blamed on the old virulent urban disease. The dispute raged all through the rest of the year with various levels of intensity. There was a recurrence in January 2002 with threats from the Protestant Red Hand Defenders that they would target members of staff. These threats were never acted upon perhaps because of promises of protection made by Ronnie Flanagan (b. 1949), the first chief constable of the new PSNI. Ardoyne has been relatively quiet since this but the existence of such pockets of tribalism is a reminder of the potential that they still have for mutual hatred and violence.

And of the future? A wiser prophet might risk soothsaying but when we consider the trauma suffered by the place for nearly four decades and the labyrinthine twists and turns that seem a necessary part of Irish political history most people will adopt the motto made famous by the shaky liberal, HH Asquith: 'Wait and see.' Some who study metaphorical entrails are filled with a kind of existential gloom but those with nothing but optimism to help them make it through the night are more at ease.

A very positive message was sent by the successful and popular mayoralty of Sinn Féin's Alex Maskey (b. 1952) in 2002–3, a term of office which caused many to blink, not to say swallow hard. The apparent rapprochement between Paisley and McGuinness, as first and second ministers, was almost surreal and their obvious appreciation of each other's sense of humour was grating to many observers. One disaffected member of the DUP described them as the 'Chuckle Brothers', a reference to well-known clowns from children's television, but to paraphrase Winston Churchill, 'Haw-haw is better than jaw-jaw is immensely better than war-war.' Paisley's subsequent passing the baton to his stalwart party colleague, Peter Robinson, did not result in any perceptible frosting in relations between the DUP and Sinn Féin, and although many hurdles remain to be negotiated between all parties, much optimism for success is evident in Belfast and beyond.

Meanwhile the increasingly elegant city is firmly out of the swamp and gaining in confidence every hour. The Opera House has moved sideways to include the Hippodrome site, the Waterfront and the Odyssey have lit up the west and east banks of the Lagan, and the Titanic Quarter will soon be a Titanic Whole. Cinema has returned multiplexly and the Arts Council of Northern Ireland has tried to be amenable to the aesthetic needs of the whole population. The city doth like a garment wear the beauty of a new beginning. It was always beautifully situated but now the stone, so long rather ugly, is becoming worthy of its setting. The gantries no longer like crucifixes stand, and the city that has never lost its air of a big market town can now risk losing watchfulness again and revert to its former proverbial friendliness.

NOTES, SELECT BIBLIOGRAPHY AND INDEX

NOTES ON THE TEXT

Chapter 1

[1]MacArt's fort was the peak of Cave Hill, known in Irish as *Beann Mhadagháin*, after a ninth-century Ulster king, and Lisnagarvagh (*Lios na cCearrbhach* or 'Fort of the Gamblers') the town land that holds the modern city of Lisburn.

Chapter 2

[1]Catholics were not even considered worthy of notice, an attitude summed up in 1714 by the Lord Chancellor of George I (1660–1727): '…the law does not suppose any such person to exist as an Irish Roman Catholic'.

[2]A term in use from the eighteenth century for the thousands of Irishmen and women who found employment with the Catholic armies of Europe from the sixteenth to the eighteenth centuries.

Chapter 3

[1]His name is also preserved in Pottinger's Entry and Pottinger's Court in Ann Street and High Street.

Chapter 4

[1]0K (or zero Kelvin) is the temperature at 'absolute zero'.

[2]In this discussion of the fortunes of the Irish language in Belfast I have used the contemporary spelling.

Chapter 5

[1]Another such was Walter Wilson who had been with Hickson from 1857. He became a vital part of Harland & Wolff with such contributions to modern design as the single-plate rudder and the use of electric current to reduce corrosion.

Chapter 6

[1]The term 'chapel' for a Catholic place of worship, used unselfconsciously by Catholics themselves, was, as we have seen, legacy of eighteenth-century practice. The word, correctly signifying an inner or subordinate place of worship, was accepted by dissenters for their churches and may still be heard.

[2]In 1905 there were nine Catholics in the employ of Belfast Corporation out of a total of 446 workers.

Chapter 7

[1] The word 'Taig' had become an alternative label for Catholic/Nationalist at the time of the first Home Rule Bill (1886), joining Papists, Fenians (in the 1860s), and the most offensive, 'Popehead'. It came from the Irish forename Tadhg, taken as the equivalent of the biblical name, Timothy. In the form Teague it became a standard name for a 'Hibernian' servant in post-Restoration drama. It was the most convenient hate word for the graffiti that decorated Belfast walls during the height of the Troubles, of which the least offensive was 'Taigs Out!'

[2] Duodecimo, in the days before International Standard paper sizes, was the smallest size of book page, and Demosthenes (384–322 BC) was the greatest of the Athenian orators.

Chapter 9

[1] In the culture of the time, 234,046 women signed their own separate document, the majority in the Ulster Hall.

[2] There was no conscription in Ireland, though Lloyd George tried to introduce it in April 1918 to counter the German spring offensive. He was forced to drop the idea by 20 June because of many protests by Nationalists throughout Ireland.

[3] Kettle immediately volunteered for service in France and was killed at Ginchy on the Somme on 9 September.

[4] The acronyms 'Fatlad' and 'Fatdad' are derived from the first letter of each of the counties involved: Fermanagh, Antrim, Tyrone, Londonderry/Derry, Armagh and Down

Chapter 10

[1] Its commander in Fermanagh, Sir Basil Brooke (1888–1975), later prime minister, proved to be a true heir of Craig by holding fast to inflexible Unionism.

[2] The Russian word *pogrom*, meaning essentially 'massacre', was used to describe the Cossacks' murderous attacks on Russian Jews from 1881, and it seemed appropriate to describe the treatment of Belfast Catholics.

Chapter 11

[1] The fear that somehow Northern Ireland's position might be modified caused Craigavon to call a general election on 9 February 1938 and 'the one politician who can fight an election without leaving his fireside', as the *Daily Express* described him, kept his overall majority of thirty-nine seats over thirteen, only one of them Labour.

Chapter 12

[1] William Beveridge (1879–1963) had written the report that became the blueprint for the Welfare Society.

[2] His oratory was formally anti-Catholic and specifically anti-papal, claiming that 'This Romish man-of-sin is now in Hell.'

[3] Ironically, the attacks were blamed on the resurgent IRA.

[4] A tribunal of inquiry under the chairmanship of Lord Saville of Newdigate (b. 1936) set up in 1998 by Tony Blair (b. 1953) and his secretary of state Mo Mowlam (1949–2005) published its findings, after much expenditure on legal fees, in 2011.

Chapter 13

[1] The UVF had, however, been busy on 17 May, with bombs in Monaghan killing seven people, and in Dublin killing twenty-six and seriously wounding a hundred.

[2] The Irish National Liberation Army (INLA) had been formed in 1975 by members of the OIRA who were dismayed at the Stickies' ceasefire. They soon acquired a reputation for ruthlessness, and the associated political arm, the Irish Republican Socialist Party (IRSP), gave rise to a rare shaft of release humour. Its greatest concentration of support was in the Lower Falls area, especially in the Divis Street tower blocks, which became known as the 'Planet of the Irps', a wordplay on the 1968 film *Planet of the Apes*.

Select Bibliography

(ed) Adams, JRR. *Merchants in Plenty – Joseph Smyth's Belfast Directory 1807–8.* Belfast: 1991

Bardon, Jonathan. *Belfast – An Illustrated History.* Belfast: 1982

———. *A History of Ulster.* Belfast: 1992

———. *Belfast – A Century.* Belfast: 1999

(eds) Beckett, JC & Glasslock, RE. *Belfast – The Origin and Growth of an Industrial City.* London: 1967

Beckett, JC et al. *Belfast – The Making of a City.* Belfast: 1983

Bell, Sam Hanna. *The Theatre in Ulster.* Dublin: 1972

Blackstock, Allan. *Double Traitors – The Belfast Volunteers and Yeomen.* Belfast: 2000

Blayney, Roger. *Belfast – 100 Years of Public Health.* Belfast: 1988

Bradbury, John. *Celebrated Citizens of Belfast.* Belfast: 2002

Brett, CEB. *Long Shadows Cast Before – Nine Lives in Ulster 1625–1977.* Edinburgh: 1978

Buckland, Patrick. *James Craig, Lord Craigavon.* Dublin: 1980

Byrne, Ophelia. *The Stage in Ulster from the Eighteenth Century.* Belfast: 1997

Cadwallader, Anne. *Holy Cross.* Belfast: 2004

(ed) Clarke, Howard B. *Irish Cities.* Cork: 1995

(ed) De Brún, Fionntán. *Belfast and the Irish Language.* Dublin: 2006

Doherty, JE & Hickey, DJ. *A Chronology of Irish History since 1500.* Dublin: 1989

Elliott, Marianne. *The Catholics of Ulster.* London: 2000

(ed) Gallagher, C. *All around the Loney-O.* Belfast: 1978

Gribbon, Sybil. *Edwardian Belfast –A Social Profile.* Belfast:1982

Hepburn, AC. *A Past Apart – Studies in the History of Catholic Belfast 1850–1950.* Belfast: 1996

Killen, John. *John Bull's Famous Circus – Ulster History through the Postcard 1905–1985*. Dublin: 1985

———. *A History of the Linen Hall Library 1788–1988*. Belfast: 1990

Lynch, Robert. *The Northern IRA and the Early Years of Partition*. Dublin: 2006

(ed) Mac Cuarta, Brian. *Ulster 1641 – Aspects of the Rising*. Belfast: 1997

MacCartan, Hugh A. *The Charm of Belfast*. Dublin: 1921

Macaulay, Ambrose. *Patrick Dorrian, Bishop of Down and Connor*. Dublin: 1987

———. *William Crolly, Archbishop of Armagh 1835–49*. Dublin: 1994

MacLoughlin, Adrian. *The City of Belfast*. Dublin: 1982

Maguire, WA. *Belfast*. Keele: 1993

Nesbitt, Noel. *The Changing Face of Belfast*. Belfast: 1968

Newmann, Kate. *Dictionary of Ulster Biography*. Belfast: 1993

Ó Buachalla, Breandán. *I mBéal Feirste cois Cuain*. Dublin: 1968

O'Byrne, Cathal. *As I Roved Out*. Belfast: 1946

(ed) Póirtéir, Cathal. *The Great Rebellion of 1798*. Cork: 1998

Pollock, Vivienne & Parkhill, Trevor. *Belfast*. Belfast: 1997

———. *A Century of Belfast*. Swindon: 2001

(ed) Roebuck, Peter. *Plantation to Partition*. Belfast: 1987

Stewart, ATQ. *The Ulster Crisis – Resistance to Home Rule 1912–1914*. London: 1967

———. *The Narrow Ground – Aspects of Ulster 1609–1969*. London: 1977

———. *Edward Carson*. Dublin: 1981

The Honest Ulsterman No 64: 'The War Years in Ulster 1939–45'. Belfast: September 1979/January 1980

Wall, Maureen. *Catholic Ireland in the Eighteenth Century*. Dublin: 1989

(ed) Young, Robert M. *The Town Book of the Corporation of Belfast*. Belfast: 1892

Index